Table of Contents

Chapter 1: Introduction to Machine Learning with Python 1

Section 1.1: What is Machine Learning?...1

The Fundamentals of Machine Learning...1

Types of Machine Learning...1

Key Applications of Machine Learning 2

Section 1.2: Why Python for Machine Learning?..2

Key Reasons to Choose Python for Machine Learning..................................3

Section 1.3: Setting Up Your Python Environment...4

Choose a Python Distribution 5

Virtual Environments..5

Package Management..5

Integrated Development Environments (IDEs) 6

Section 1.4: Python Basics for Machine Learning 7

Variables and Data Types 7

Control Structures...7

Functions 7

Lists and Iteration...7

NumPy for Numerical Operations...8

Pandas for Data Manipulation 8

Matplotlib for Data Visualization 8

Getting Help and Documentation...9

Python in Jupyter Notebooks...9

Section 1.5: Common Libraries for Machine Learning in Python 9

1. NumPy..9

2. Pandas 10

3. Scikit-Learn 10

4. Matplotlib and Seaborn...11

5. TensorFlow and PyTorch..11

6. Jupyter Notebooks...12

Chapter 2: Data Preprocessing and Exploration...13

Section 2.1: Data Cleaning and Imputation 13

Data Cleaning...13

Data Imputation 13

Section 2.2: Data Transformation and Scaling..14

Data Transformation...15

Data Scaling...15

When to Apply Data Transformation and Scaling..16

Section 2.3: Exploratory Data Analysis (EDA) 17

The Goals of EDA...17

Common EDA Techniques 17

Iterative Process 18

Section 2.4: Feature Engineering...19

The Importance of Feature Engineering 19

Common Feature Engineering Techniques 19

The Role of Domain Knowledge..20

Iterative Process 20

Section 2.5: Handling Categorical Data 21

Types of Categorical Data 21

Techniques for Handling Categorical Data...21

Handling High Cardinality 22

Dealing with Missing Data in Categorical Variables..22

Chapter 3: Supervised Learning: Regression 24

Section 3.1: Understanding Regression...24

What is Regression? 24

Applications of Regression 24

Types of Regression..24

Model Evaluation in Regression..25

Section 3.2: Simple Linear Regression 26

The Simple Linear Regression Model 26

Estimating the Coefficients..26

Implementing Simple Linear Regression in Python...27

Model Evaluation in Simple Linear Regression..28

Section 3.3: Multiple Linear Regression 28

The Multiple Linear Regression Model 28

Estimating the Coefficients..28

Implementing Multiple Linear Regression in Python..29

Model Evaluation in Multiple Linear Regression...30

Section 3.4: Polynomial Regression 30

The Polynomial Regression Model..30

Estimating the Coefficients..30

Implementing Polynomial Regression in Python 31

Model Evaluation in Polynomial Regression 32

Section 3.5: Evaluation Metrics for Regression Models...32

1. Mean Absolute Error (MAE) 32

2. Mean Squared Error (MSE) 32

3. Root Mean Squared Error (RMSE) 33

4. R-squared (R2) 33

Choosing the Right Evaluation Metric 33

Chapter 4: Supervised Learning: Classification 35

Section 4.1: Introduction to Classification...35

What is Classification?..35

Applications of Classification 35

Types of Classification..35

Model Evaluation in Classification 36

Section 4.2: Logistic Regression...36

Understanding Logistic Regression..37

Estimating Coefficients 37

Implementing Logistic Regression in Python 37

Model Evaluation in Logistic Regression 38

Section 4.3: Decision Trees and Random Forests 38

Decision Trees...38

Random Forests 39

Implementing Decision Trees and Random Forests in Python 39

Model Evaluation in Decision Trees and Random Forests 41

Section 4.4: Support Vector Machines (SVM)..41

Understanding Support Vector Machines..41

Hyperparameter Tuning...41

Implementing SVM in Python 42

Model Evaluation in SVM 43

Section 4.5: Evaluation Metrics for Classification Models...43

Accuracy 43

Precision 43

Recall (Sensitivity or True Positive Rate) 43

F1 Score 44

Specificity (True Negative Rate) 44

Receiver Operating Characteristic (ROC) Curve and Area Under the Curve (AUC) ...44

Confusion Matrix..44

Cross-Validation...44

Choosing the Right Metric...44

Chapter 5: Unsupervised Learning: Clustering 46

Section 5.1: Clustering Concepts..46

What is Clustering?...46

Key Concepts in Clustering..46

Evaluation of Clustering 47

Applications of Clustering...47

Section 5.2: K-Means Clustering 47

How K-Means Clustering Works...48

Choosing the Number of Clusters (k)..48

K-Means Implementation in Python 48

Applications of K-Means Clustering 49

Section 5.3: Hierarchical Clustering...50

How Hierarchical Clustering Works..50

Types of Hierarchical Clustering..50

Linkage Methods..50

Dendrogram Cutting...51

Hierarchical Clustering Implementation in Python..51

Applications of Hierarchical Clustering 52

Section 5.4: Density-Based Clustering..52

How DBSCAN Works...52

DBSCAN Implementation in Python...53

Advantages and Limitations of DBSCAN 53

Applications of DBSCAN 54

Section 5.5: Evaluating Clustering Performance 54

Internal Evaluation Metrics 54

External Evaluation Metrics...55

Visual Evaluation 55

Limitations of Evaluation Metrics 55

Choosing the Right Metric..56

Chapter 6: Dimensionality Reduction 57

Section 6.1: Why Dimensionality Reduction? 57

1. Curse of Dimensionality..57

2. Improved Model Performance 57

3. Enhanced Visualization..57

4. Faster Training and Inference..57

5. Noise Reduction 57

6. Feature Engineering...58

7. Interpretability 58

8. Data Compression 58

9. Preprocessing for Downstream Tasks...58

Section 6.2: Principal Component Analysis (PCA) 58

Key Concepts 58

PCA Implementation in Python...59

Applications of PCA 59

Limitations of PCA...60

Section 6.3: t-Distributed Stochastic Neighbor Embedding (t-SNE)......................................60

Key Concepts 60

t-SNE Implementation in Python...61

Applications of t-SNE 61

Limitations of t-SNE 62

Section 6.4: Linear Discriminant Analysis (LDA) 62

Key Concepts 62

LDA Implementation in Python..63

Applications of LDA 63

Limitations of LDA 64

Section 6.5: Applications of Dimensionality Reduction..64

Data Visualization..64

Noise Reduction 65

Feature Engineering...65

Preprocessing for Machine Learning...65

Anomaly Detection..65

Computational Efficiency..65

Limitations and Considerations...65

Chapter 7: Model Selection and Hyperparameter Tuning..67

Section 7.1: Cross-Validation Techniques 67

The Need for Cross-Validation...67

Cross-Validation Overview...67

Benefits of Cross-Validation..68

Choosing the Right Cross-Validation Technique 68

Section 7.2: Grid Search and Random Search 68

Grid Search...69

Random Search..69

Grid Search vs. Random Search..70

Section 7.3: Hyperparameter Tuning Best Practices 71

1. Start with a Coarse Search:...71

2. Use Prior Knowledge: 71

3. Use Validation Data: 71

4. Implement Early Stopping:..71

5. Logarithmic Scales for Parameters:..71

6. Ensemble of Models:...71

7. Random Search After Grid Search:...72

8. Use Specialized Libraries: 72

9. Consider Bayesian Optimization:..72

10. Parallelize the Search:..72

11. Track and Visualize Results:..72

12. Regularize Models: 72

13. Evaluate on a Held-Out Test Set: 72

14. Iterate as Necessary:..72

15. Documentation: 72

Section 7.4: Model Evaluation and Selection..73

1. Performance Metrics:..73

2. Cross-Validation:...73

3. Hold-Out Validation Set: 73

4. Model Comparison:...73

5. Overfitting and Underfitting:...73

6. Bias-Variance Tradeoff:...73

7. Ensemble Methods:..73

8. Interpretability:...74

9. Regularization:..74

10. Final Test Set:..74

11. Model Robustness:...74

12. Business Objectives:..74

13. Iterative Process:...74

14. Documentation:...74

Section 7.5: Avoiding Overfitting and Underfitting.................................74

Overfitting:...75

Underfitting:...75

Chapter 8: Ensemble Learning...76

Section 8.1: Ensemble Methods Overview..76

Section 8.2: Bagging: Bootstrap Aggregating..78

How Bagging Works:...78

Benefits of Bagging:...78

Example Implementation in Python:...79

Section 8.3: Boosting: AdaBoost and Gradient Boosting.........................79

AdaBoost (Adaptive Boosting):..79

Gradient Boosting:...80

Example Implementation in Python:...80

Section 8.4: Stacking and Blending..81

Stacking:..81

Blending:..81

Benefits and Considerations:...82

Example Implementation in Python:...82

Section 8.5: Building Robust Models with Ensembles..............................83

Robustness in Machine Learning:...83

Ensemble Strategies for Robustness:...84

Example Implementation in Python:...84

Chapter 9: Neural Networks and Deep Learning......................................86

Section 9.1: Introduction to Neural Networks...86

    Key Concepts:...86

    Types of Neural Networks:...87

Section 9.2: Building a Neural Network in Python 87

    Importing Libraries:...87

    Building the Neural Network: 88

    Customizing the Architecture: 88

    Saving and Loading Models: 89

Section 9.3: Convolutional Neural Networks (CNNs) 89

    Key Components of CNNs: 89

    CNN Architecture: 90

    Training CNNs:...90

    Transfer Learning: 90

    Applications of CNNs: 90

Section 9.4: Recurrent Neural Networks (RNNs)...91

    Key Components of RNNs:..91

    RNN Architectures:...92

    Training RNNs: 92

    Challenges with RNNs: 92

    Applications of RNNs:...92

Section 9.5: Deep Learning Applications...93

    1. Computer Vision: 93

    2. Natural Language Processing (NLP): 93

    3. Reinforcement Learning:..94

    4. Healthcare:..94

    5. Autonomous Vehicles: 94

Chapter 10: Natural Language Processing with Python..96

Section 10.1: Text Preprocessing and Tokenization 96

    Why Text Preprocessing?..96

    Tokenization Techniques..96

    Conclusion 97

Section 10.2: Building Text Classification Models...97

    Data Preparation...98

    Text Vectorization 98

Model Selection 98

Model Evaluation..99

Conclusion 99

Section 10.3: Word Embeddings (Word2Vec, GloVe)................................100

Word2Vec..100

GloVe (Global Vectors for Word Representation) 100

Application of Word Embeddings..101

Conclusion..101

Section 10.4: Sequence-to-Sequence Models................................102

Architecture of Seq2Seq Models 102

Applications of Seq2Seq Models..102

Example Code 103

Section 10.5: Sentiment Analysis and Text Generation 104

Sentiment Analysis..104

Text Generation 104

Example Code 105

Chapter 11: Computer Vision with Python................................106

Section 11.1: Image Data Handling in Python 106

Section 11.2: Image Classification 108

Understanding Image Classification 108

Implementing Image Classification..108

Conclusion..109

Section 11.3: Object Detection and Localization 110

Understanding Object Detection 110

Techniques for Object Detection..110

Implementing Object Detection..111

Object Detection Tools..111

Section 11.4: Transfer Learning with Pretrained Models................112

The Motivation for Transfer Learning..112

Fine-Tuning Pretrained Models..112

Popular Object Detection Frameworks 113

Section 11.5: Advanced Computer Vision Applications................113

1. Medical Image Analysis 113

2. Autonomous Vehicles..114

3. Agriculture and Precision Farming 114

4. Retail and E-commerce 114

5. Security and Surveillance 114

6. Augmented Reality (AR) and Virtual Reality (VR) 114

7. Environmental Monitoring 114

8. Quality Control and Manufacturing 114

Chapter 12: Time Series Analysis and Forecasting 116

Section 12.1: Time Series Data Handling 116

What is Time Series Data? 116

Time Series Data Components 116

Data Visualization 116

Time Indexing 116

Data Preprocessing 117

Libraries for Time Series Analysis 117

Section 12.2: Time Series Decomposition 117

Understanding Time Series Decomposition 117

Additive vs. Multiplicative Decomposition 118

Decomposition Using Python 118

Section 12.3: ARIMA Models for Time Series Forecasting 119

Components of ARIMA Models 119

Building ARIMA Models in Python 119

Section 12.4: Prophet for Time Series Forecasting 121

Key Features of Prophet 121

Building Prophet Models in Python 121

Section 12.5: Evaluating Time Series Models 122

Key Metrics for Time Series Evaluation 123

Cross-Validation for Time Series 123

Visualizing Forecasts 124

Chapter 13: Reinforcement Learning 125

Section 13.1: Introduction to Reinforcement Learning 125

Key Concepts in Reinforcement Learning 125

Reinforcement Learning Workflow 126

Applications of Reinforcement Learning 126

Section 13.2: Q-Learning 127

Key Concepts in Q-Learning..127

Q-Learning Algorithm...128

Pseudocode..128

Applications of Q-Learning...128

Section 13.3: Deep Q-Networks (DQN) 129

Key Concepts in Deep Q-Networks 129

DQN Algorithm...129

Pseudocode..130

Applications of DQN...130

Section 13.4: Policy Gradients..131

Key Concepts in Policy Gradients 131

Policy Gradient Algorithm..132

Advantages of Policy Gradients 132

Challenges of Policy Gradients 132

Section 13.5: Real-World Applications of Reinforcement Learning.................133

1. Game Playing: 133

2. Robotics: 133

3. Autonomous Vehicles: 133

4. Healthcare:..133

5. Finance: 133

6. Recommendation Systems:...133

7. Natural Language Processing (NLP):..133

8. Supply Chain Management: 134

9. Energy Management:...134

10. Game Development: 134

Challenges and Future Directions: 134

Chapter 14: Model Deployment and Serving..135

Section 14.1: Exporting Machine Learning Models..135

Why Exporting Matters 135

Common Model Export Formats 135

Exporting a Model in Python 135

Section 14.2: Building RESTful APIs with Flask 136

Why Use Flask for API Development...136

Setting Up Flask..137

Creating an API Endpoint for Model Prediction 137

Running the Flask API...138

Section 14.3: Containerization with Docker 138

Why Use Docker for Model Deployment..138

Creating a Dockerfile 139

Building and Running the Docker Container 139

Deploying to the Cloud with Docker..140

Section 14.4: Cloud Deployment (AWS, Azure, GCP) 140

AWS Deployment...140

Azure Deployment...140

GCP Deployment..141

Choosing the Right Cloud Provider 141

Section 14.5: Monitoring and Scaling Models in Production...................................142

Monitoring Machine Learning Models..143

Scaling Machine Learning Models 143

Continuous Improvement...144

Chapter 15: Ethics and Bias in Machine Learning..145

Section 15.1: Understanding Bias and Fairness 145

What is Bias?..145

Types of Bias 145

Impact of Bias 145

Fairness in Machine Learning 146

Section 15.2: Ethical Considerations in Machine Learning 146

Data Privacy 146

Transparency and Explainability...146

Accountability and Bias Mitigation 146

Fairness and Non-Discrimination..147

Ethical Decision-Making 147

Case Studies on Ethical Dilemmas..147

Section 15.3: Bias Mitigation Techniques 147

1. Data Preprocessing 148

2. Algorithmic Techniques 148

3. Post-processing Techniques...148

4. Fairness Metrics 148

5. Continuous Monitoring...149

6. Ethical Review Boards 149

7. Bias Audits 149

8. User Feedback 149

9. Diversity in Development Teams..149

Section 15.4: Responsible AI Development..149

1. Data Privacy and Security 149

2. Transparency and Explainability 150

3. Fairness and Bias Mitigation...150

4. Accountability and Governance...150

5. User-Centric Design 150

6. Accountability for Outcomes...151

7. Ethical Considerations...151

8. Public Engagement..151

9. Continuous Learning and Improvement..151

Section 15.5: Case Studies on Ethical Dilemmas...152

Case Study 1: Predictive Policing Bias...152

Case Study 2: Automated Hiring Algorithms 152

Case Study 3: Autonomous Vehicles and Moral Dilemmas..........................152

Case Study 4: Deepfake Technology 153

Case Study 5: AI in Healthcare Diagnosis..153

Case Study 6: Social Media Algorithms and Polarization 153

Chapter 16: Real-World Machine Learning Projects.....................................154

Section 16.1: Project Development Lifecycle...154

The Machine Learning Project Lifecycle...154

Collaboration and Documentation 155

Project Management Tools 155

Ethical Considerations...155

Section 16.2: Choosing the Right Project..155

1. Business Impact...155

2. Data Availability 156

3. Project Complexity 156

4. Ethical and Regulatory Considerations 156

5. Project Resources 156

6. Return on Investment (ROI)..156

7. Alignment with User Needs..157

8. Scalability and Deployment..157

9. Alignment with Machine Learning Capabilities...157

10. Alignment with Organizational Culture..157

Section 16.3: Data Collection and Annotation...157

The Importance of Data Collection..157

Methods of Data Collection...158

Data Annotation 158

Tools and Platforms...159

Section 16.4: Building and Iterating Models...159

Model Development..159

Model Evaluation and Refinement...160

Conclusion..161

Section 16.5: Deployment and Maintenance 161

Deployment Considerations...161

Containerization with Docker 162

Cloud Deployment..163

Monitoring and Scaling...163

Conclusion..164

Chapter 17: Case Studies in Industry...165

Section 17.1: Machine Learning in Healthcare 165

Electronic Health Records (EHR)...165

Medical Imaging 165

Drug Discovery and Genomics 166

Telemedicine and Remote Monitoring...166

Ethical Considerations...167

Section 17.2: Financial Services and Risk Assessment...167

Credit Risk Assessment...167

Fraud Detection...168

Algorithmic Trading 168

Regulatory Compliance 168

Ethical Considerations...169

Section 17.3: E-commerce and Recommendation Systems.....................................169

Personalized Product Recommendations 169

Content-Based Recommendations 170

Real-Time Recommendations 170

Upselling and Cross-Selling 171

Ethical Considerations 171

Section 17.4: Autonomous Vehicles and Robotics..171

Self-Driving Cars...171

Robotics and Automation..172

Ethical Considerations 173

Section 17.5: Impact of ML on Various Industries 173

Healthcare 173

Financial Services 174

E-commerce 174

Manufacturing...174

Transportation and Logistics..174

Entertainment and Media 174

Agriculture..175

Chapter 18: Future Trends in Machine Learning..175

Section 18.1: Current Trends and Challenges 175

Section 18.2: Explainable AI (XAI) 176

Importance of Explainable AI 177

XAI Techniques 177

Challenges and Trade-Offs 178

Section 18.3: Quantum Machine Learning..178

Key Concepts in Quantum Computing..178

Applications of Quantum Machine Learning...179

Challenges and Limitations 179

Future Directions...180

Section 18.4: Federated Learning..180

How Federated Learning Works 180

Privacy and Security Benefits...181

Applications of Federated Learning 181

Challenges and Considerations...181

Future Directions...182

Section 18.5: Ethical AI and Regulation 182

Ethical Considerations in AI 182

Responsible AI Development 183

Role of Regulation 183

Challenges and Future Directions 184

Section 19.1: Books, Courses, and Online Resources 185

Books 185

Online Courses 185

Online Resources 186

Section 19.2: Joining Machine Learning Communities 186

1. Reddit's Machine Learning Community (r/MachineLearning) 187

2. LinkedIn Groups 187

3. Meetup and Event Platforms 187

4. GitHub 187

5. Online Forums and Q&A Platforms 187

6. Kaggle Community 187

7. AI and ML Conferences 188

8. Online Learning Platforms 188

9. Social Media 188

Section 19.3: Keeping Up with the Latest Research 188

1. ArXiv and Preprint Servers 188

2. Academic Journals 189

3. Conferences and Workshops 189

4. ResearchGate and Google Scholar 189

5. Blogs and Newsletters 189

6. Podcasts and YouTube Channels 189

7. Social Media and Online Communities 189

8. Research Labs and Organizations 189

9. Online Courses and Specializations 189

10. Peer Discussion Groups 190

Section 19.4: Building Your Machine Learning Portfolio 190

1. Select Diverse Projects 190

2. Highlight Real-World Applications 190

3. Provide Clear Documentation 190

4. Share Code Repositories 191

5. Display Visualizations and Results..191

6. Explain Your Process..191

7. Showcase Model Performance 191

8. Include Personal Projects 191

9. Share Challenges and Learning..191

10. Keep It Updated..191

11. Seek Feedback 191

12. Make It Accessible...192

13. Personalize Your Story..192

Section 19.5: Career Opportunities in Machine Learning.....................................192

1. Machine Learning Engineer...192

2. Data Scientist 192

3. AI Researcher...192

4. Natural Language Processing (NLP) Engineer 193

5. Computer Vision Engineer 193

6. Data Engineer 193

7. AI Product Manager 193

8. Machine Learning Operations (MLOps) Engineer 193

9. AI Ethics and Fairness Researcher 193

10. Industry-Specific Roles 193

11. Start Your Own Venture 194

12. Academia and Research Institutions 194

13. Freelancing and Consulting 194

14. Government and Nonprofits..194

15. Continuous Learning and Networking..194

Chapter 20: Conclusion and Beyond 194

Section 20.1: Recap of the Journey...194

Key Takeaways 196

Embracing a Lifelong Learning Mindset..197

**Your Role...197

Section 20.2: Key Takeaways 197

Section 20.3: Embracing a Lifelong Learning Mindset...198

1. Continuous Learning Is Essential..198

2. Stay Informed About Industry Trends...198

3. Contribute to Open Source Projects..198

4. Collaborate and Network..199

5. Mentorship and Teaching...199

6. Experiment and Innovate...199

7. Ethical Considerations 199

8. Portfolio Development..199

9. Career Advancement 199

10. Impact on Society 199

Section 20.4: Your Role in Advancing AI and ML.................................200

1. Problem Solving with AI/ML 200

2. Research and Innovation..200

3. Education and Mentorship..200

4. Ethical Leadership 200

5. Interdisciplinary Collaboration 200

6. Open Source Contributions..200

7. Diverse and Inclusive AI..201

8. Advocacy and Policy 201

9. Real-World Applications...201

10. Lifelong Learning...201

Section 20.5: Looking Ahead to the Future of ML................................201

1. Explainable AI (XAI)...201

2. Quantum Machine Learning...201

3. Federated Learning..202

4. Ethical AI and Regulation 202

5. AutoML and Democratization..202

6. Natural Language Processing Advancements...................................202

7. AI in Healthcare 202

8. AI in Climate Science 202

9. AI in Robotics and Autonomous Systems...202

10. AI for Social Good 202

11. Human-Machine Collaboration 203

12. Edge AI 203

13. Continuous Learning..203

14. AI in Creativity..203
15. Global Collaboration 203

Chapter 1: Introduction to Machine Learning with Python

Section 1.1: What is Machine Learning?

Machine Learning (ML) is a subfield of artificial intelligence (AI) that focuses on the development of algorithms and statistical models that enable computers to learn and make predictions or decisions without being explicitly programmed. In traditional programming, humans write explicit instructions for a computer to perform specific tasks. However, in machine learning, the computer learns from data and experiences to improve its performance on a particular task.

The Fundamentals of Machine Learning

At its core, machine learning revolves around the concept of learning from data. This learning process involves the following key elements:

1. **Data:** Machine learning algorithms require data as input. This data can take various forms, such as text, images, numerical values, or even more complex structures like graphs. Data serves as the foundation for training and testing machine learning models.

2. **Features:** Within the data, we identify features, which are specific attributes or characteristics that the model uses to make predictions. For example, in a spam email classification task, features might include the presence of certain keywords or the sender's email address.

3. **Model:** The machine learning model is the algorithm or mathematical function that learns patterns and relationships within the data. It uses these patterns to make predictions or decisions. The model's parameters are adjusted during training to minimize prediction errors.

4. **Training:** During the training phase, the model is exposed to a labeled dataset, where the correct outcomes or labels are known. The model learns to make predictions by adjusting its internal parameters based on the input data and comparing its predictions to the true labels.

5. **Testing and Evaluation:** After training, the model's performance is evaluated using a separate dataset that it has never seen before. This helps assess how well the model generalizes to new, unseen data.

Types of Machine Learning

Machine learning can be broadly categorized into three main types:

1. **Supervised Learning:** In supervised learning, the model is trained on a labeled dataset, where each example has a known output or target variable. The goal is to learn a mapping from input features to the target variable, making it suitable for tasks like classification and regression.

2. **Unsupervised Learning:** Unsupervised learning deals with unlabeled data, where the model aims to discover hidden patterns or structures within the data. Clustering and dimensionality reduction are common tasks in unsupervised learning.

3. **Reinforcement Learning:** Reinforcement learning is concerned with training agents to make sequences of decisions in an environment to maximize a cumulative reward. It is widely used in applications like game playing, robotics, and autonomous systems.

Key Applications of Machine Learning

Machine learning has a wide range of applications across various domains:

- **Natural Language Processing (NLP):** ML is used for tasks like text classification, sentiment analysis, language translation, and chatbots.
- **Computer Vision:** ML is applied to image and video analysis, including object detection, facial recognition, and autonomous driving.
- **Healthcare:** ML aids in medical diagnosis, drug discovery, and personalized treatment recommendations.
- **Finance:** ML is used for fraud detection, credit scoring, and stock price forecasting.
- **Recommendation Systems:** ML powers recommendation engines in e-commerce and content platforms.
- **Industrial Automation:** ML is used for predictive maintenance, quality control, and supply chain optimization.

Machine learning continues to evolve and has a profound impact on various industries, making it a crucial field for both research and practical applications. As we delve deeper into this book, you will gain a comprehensive understanding of the principles, techniques, and tools used in machine learning, with a focus on Python as the primary programming language.

Section 1.2: Why Python for Machine Learning?

Python has emerged as one of the most popular programming languages for machine learning, and for good reason. Its simplicity, versatility, and extensive libraries make it an ideal choice for both beginners and experienced data scientists and machine learning practitioners.

Key Reasons to Choose Python for Machine Learning

1. Readability and Simplicity:

Python is known for its clean and readable syntax, which resembles the English language. This readability makes it easier to write, understand, and maintain code. It's an excellent language for beginners because it emphasizes code clarity and reduces the learning curve.

```
# Example of Python's readability
if age >= 18:
    print("You are eligible to vote.")
else:
    print("You are not eligible to vote.")
```

2. Extensive Libraries and Frameworks:

Python boasts a rich ecosystem of libraries and frameworks specifically designed for machine learning and data science. Some of the most popular ones include:

- **NumPy:** A library for numerical computations, providing support for multi-dimensional arrays and matrices.
- **Pandas:** A data manipulation and analysis library that simplifies working with structured data.
- **Scikit-Learn:** A comprehensive machine learning library that includes various algorithms and tools for classification, regression, clustering, and more.
- **TensorFlow and PyTorch:** Deep learning frameworks that facilitate the creation and training of neural networks.
- **Matplotlib and Seaborn:** Libraries for data visualization, essential for understanding and presenting results.

These libraries streamline various tasks in the machine learning pipeline, from data preprocessing to model building and evaluation.

3. Community Support and Documentation:

Python has a vast and active user community. This means you can easily find solutions to common problems, access tutorials, and seek help from forums and communities. The availability of extensive documentation for libraries and frameworks makes it easier to learn and use them effectively.

4. Cross-Platform Compatibility:

Python is cross-platform, meaning you can develop machine learning applications on different operating systems, such as Windows, macOS, and Linux, without major compatibility issues. This flexibility is particularly valuable in collaborative or diverse computing environments.

5. Integration with Other Technologies:

Python can seamlessly integrate with other programming languages and technologies. This is advantageous when you need to incorporate machine learning into larger software systems or utilize specialized libraries written in other languages.

6. Rapid Prototyping and Experimentation:

Python's interactive nature and the availability of Jupyter notebooks make it perfect for rapid prototyping and experimentation. You can quickly test ideas, tweak models, and visualize results in an interactive environment.

```python
# Example of using Jupyter notebook for interactive experimentation
import pandas as pd

# Load a dataset
data = pd.read_csv('data.csv')

# Explore data interactively in a Jupyter notebook
data.head()
```

7. Support for Big Data and Cloud Computing:

Python has libraries and tools for big data processing and analysis, such as Apache Spark and Dask. Additionally, it integrates well with cloud platforms like AWS, Azure, and Google Cloud, allowing you to leverage scalable computing resources for machine learning tasks.

8. Wide Adoption in Industry:

Python's popularity in the industry has led to its widespread adoption in various domains, including finance, healthcare, tech, and more. Learning Python for machine learning can open up career opportunities and increase your marketability.

In summary, Python's simplicity, powerful libraries, active community, and versatility make it an excellent choice for machine learning. Whether you are a beginner or an experienced practitioner, Python provides the tools and resources you need to excel in the field of machine learning. This book will guide you through the journey of mastering machine learning with Python, equipping you with the skills and knowledge to tackle real-world problems effectively.

Section 1.3: Setting Up Your Python Environment

Before diving into machine learning with Python, it's essential to set up your development environment properly. A well-configured environment ensures that you can work efficiently and effectively throughout your machine learning journey. In this section, we'll cover the key components of setting up a Python environment for machine learning.

Choose a Python Distribution

Python is available in various distributions, but for machine learning, two popular choices are Anaconda and plain Python. Anaconda is a Python distribution specifically tailored for data science and machine learning. It comes with a package manager called conda, which simplifies the installation and management of libraries and environments.

To install Anaconda, follow these steps:

1. Download the Anaconda installer for your operating system from the Anaconda website.

2. Run the installer and follow the installation instructions.

3. Once installed, you can use the Anaconda Navigator graphical interface to manage packages and environments.

Virtual Environments

Using virtual environments is essential for isolating your machine learning projects and their dependencies. This prevents conflicts between different projects that may require different versions of libraries. Python provides the venv module for creating virtual environments.

Creating a Virtual Environment

To create a virtual environment, open a terminal and run the following commands:

```
# Create a new virtual environment named 'myenv'
python -m venv myenv
```

```
# Activate the virtual environment
# On Windows:
myenv\Scripts\activate
# On macOS and Linux:
source myenv/bin/activate
```

You'll see the virtual environment name in your terminal prompt, indicating that you are now working within the virtual environment.

Package Management

Managing Python packages is a crucial aspect of setting up your environment. The primary tools for package management in Python are pip and conda (if you're using Anaconda). You can use these tools to install, update, and remove packages.

Installing Packages with pip

To install a package using pip, use the following command:

```
pip install package-name
```

For example, to install the NumPy package, you would run:

```
pip install numpy
```

If you're using Anaconda, you can use conda to install packages. Conda can also create and manage virtual environments.

```
# Create a new virtual environment with conda
conda create --name myenv python=3.8

# Activate the conda virtual environment
conda activate myenv

# Install a package with conda
conda install package-name
```

Integrated Development Environments (IDEs)

While Python can be developed in any text editor, using an Integrated Development Environment (IDE) designed for data science and machine learning can significantly improve your productivity. Some popular Python IDEs for machine learning include:

- **Jupyter Notebook:** Jupyter provides an interactive environment for data analysis and machine learning experimentation. It's widely used for creating and sharing documents that contain live code, equations, visualizations, and narrative text.

- **PyCharm:** PyCharm is a powerful Python IDE that offers features like code completion, debugging, and integrated testing. The professional version includes support for data science and machine learning.

- **Visual Studio Code (VS Code):** VS Code is a lightweight, open-source code editor with a rich ecosystem of extensions. You can turn it into a powerful Python IDE by adding relevant extensions like Jupyter support.

Choose an IDE that suits your preferences and workflow, and make sure to customize it to your liking.

In this section, we've covered the fundamental steps to set up your Python environment for machine learning. By selecting the right distribution, creating virtual environments, managing packages, and choosing an appropriate IDE, you'll be well-prepared to start your machine learning projects and experiments in Python.

Section 1.4: Python Basics for Machine Learning

Before delving deeper into machine learning, it's essential to have a solid grasp of the fundamental concepts and techniques in Python. This section provides an overview of Python basics that are commonly used in machine learning workflows.

Variables and Data Types

In Python, you can assign values to variables, and the data type is dynamically inferred. Common data types include integers, floating-point numbers, strings, lists, and dictionaries.

```python
# Assigning values to variables
x = 10   # integer
y = 3.14   # float
name = "Alice"   # string
my_list = [1, 2, 3, 4]   # list
my_dict = {'key1': 'value1', 'key2': 'value2'}   # dictionary
```

Control Structures

Control structures like if, else, and for loops are essential for conditional execution and iteration.

```python
# Conditional statement
if x > 5:
    print("x is greater than 5")
else:
    print("x is not greater than 5")


# For Loop
for i in range(5):
    print(i)
```

Functions

Functions allow you to encapsulate reusable code and make your code modular.

```python
# Define a function
def greet(name):
    return f"Hello, {name}!"


# Call the function
message = greet("Alice")
print(message)
```

Lists and Iteration

Lists are ordered collections that can store elements of different data types. You can iterate over them using for loops.

```python
fruits = ['apple', 'banana', 'cherry']


# Iterate over the list
for fruit in fruits:
    print(fruit)
```

NumPy for Numerical Operations

NumPy is a fundamental library for numerical operations in Python, especially in machine learning.

```python
import numpy as np

# Create a NumPy array
arr = np.array([1, 2, 3, 4, 5])

# Perform operations on the array
mean = np.mean(arr)
print(mean)
```

Pandas for Data Manipulation

Pandas is a popular library for data manipulation and analysis. It provides data structures like DataFrames.

```python
import pandas as pd

# Create a DataFrame
data = {'Name': ['Alice', 'Bob', 'Charlie'],
        'Age': [25, 30, 35]}
df = pd.DataFrame(data)

# Access data in the DataFrame
print(df['Name'])
```

Matplotlib for Data Visualization

Matplotlib is a versatile library for creating data visualizations.

```python
import matplotlib.pyplot as plt

# Create a simple plot
x = [1, 2, 3, 4, 5]
y = [10, 20, 25, 30, 35]
plt.plot(x, y)
plt.xlabel('X-axis')
plt.ylabel('Y-axis')
plt.title('Simple Plot')
plt.show()
```

Getting Help and Documentation

You can access Python documentation and help using the help() function or by referring to online resources and tutorials. For library-specific help, refer to the documentation of the respective library.

```
# Get help for a function or object
help(len)

# Get help for a library function
help(np.mean)
```

Python in Jupyter Notebooks

Jupyter Notebooks provide an interactive environment for data exploration and analysis. They allow you to combine code, visualizations, and explanations in a single document.

```
# Jupyter cell for code execution
```

In this section, we've covered the foundational Python concepts and libraries that you'll frequently encounter when working on machine learning projects. Understanding these basics is crucial for building more complex machine learning models and data analysis workflows. As you progress through this book, you'll apply these concepts to real-world machine learning problems and gain hands-on experience.

Section 1.5: Common Libraries for Machine Learning in Python

Python's strength in machine learning lies not only in its simplicity and readability but also in its rich ecosystem of libraries and frameworks tailored for various aspects of machine learning and data science. In this section, we'll introduce some of the most commonly used libraries that you'll encounter throughout your machine learning journey.

1. NumPy

NumPy is the fundamental library for numerical computing in Python. It provides support for multi-dimensional arrays and matrices, along with a wide range of mathematical functions for performing operations on these arrays efficiently.

```
import numpy as np

# Create a NumPy array
arr = np.array([1, 2, 3, 4, 5])

# Compute the mean
mean = np.mean(arr)
print(mean)
```

NumPy is the backbone of many other libraries, including Pandas and Matplotlib, making it essential for data manipulation and analysis.

2. Pandas

Pandas is a versatile library for data manipulation and analysis. It introduces two primary data structures, Series (one-dimensional) and DataFrame (two-dimensional), that allow you to work with structured data efficiently.

```python
import pandas as pd

# Create a DataFrame
data = {'Name': ['Alice', 'Bob', 'Charlie'],
        'Age': [25, 30, 35]}
df = pd.DataFrame(data)

# Access data in the DataFrame
print(df['Name'])
```

Pandas simplifies tasks like data cleaning, transformation, and aggregation, making it a crucial tool in data preprocessing for machine learning.

3. Scikit-Learn

Scikit-Learn is a comprehensive machine learning library that provides a wide range of algorithms for tasks such as classification, regression, clustering, dimensionality reduction, and more. It offers a consistent API and extensive documentation, making it suitable for both beginners and experts.

```python
from sklearn.datasets import load_iris
from sklearn.model_selection import train_test_split
from sklearn.tree import DecisionTreeClassifier

# Load the Iris dataset
iris = load_iris()
X, y = iris.data, iris.target

# Split the data into training and testing sets
X_train, X_test, y_train, y_test = train_test_split(X, y, test_size=0.2)

# Create a Decision Tree classifier
clf = DecisionTreeClassifier()

# Train the classifier
clf.fit(X_train, y_train)
```

Scikit-Learn also includes tools for model selection, hyperparameter tuning, and evaluation metrics.

4. Matplotlib and Seaborn

Matplotlib is a popular library for creating data visualizations. It provides a wide range of plotting options for creating line plots, scatter plots, bar plots, histograms, and more.

```python
import matplotlib.pyplot as plt

# Create a simple plot
x = [1, 2, 3, 4, 5]
y = [10, 20, 25, 30, 35]
plt.plot(x, y)
plt.xlabel('X-axis')
plt.ylabel('Y-axis')
plt.title('Simple Plot')
plt.show()
```

Seaborn is built on top of Matplotlib and provides a higher-level interface for creating attractive statistical visualizations. It is particularly useful for exploring and visualizing datasets.

```python
import seaborn as sns

# Create a pair plot
sns.pairplot(df, hue='Species')
```

5. TensorFlow and PyTorch

TensorFlow and **PyTorch** are deep learning frameworks used for building and training neural networks. They offer high-level APIs for developing models and low-level APIs for customizing network architectures.

```python
import tensorflow as tf

# Create a simple neural network using TensorFlow
model = tf.keras.Sequential([
    tf.keras.layers.Dense(64, activation='relu', input_shape=(784,)),
    tf.keras.layers.Dense(10, activation='softmax')
])
```

```python
import torch
import torch.nn as nn

# Create a simple neural network using PyTorch
class Net(nn.Module):
    def __init__(self):
        super(Net, self).__init__()
        self.fc1 = nn.Linear(784, 64)
        self.fc2 = nn.Linear(64, 10)


model = Net()
```

These deep learning frameworks are widely used for tasks like image classification, natural language processing, and reinforcement learning.

6. Jupyter Notebooks

Jupyter Notebooks provide an interactive environment for data analysis and machine learning experimentation. They allow you to create and share documents that combine code, visualizations, and narrative text.

```
# Jupyter cell for code execution
```

These are just a few of the many libraries and tools available in the Python ecosystem for machine learning. As you progress in your machine learning journey, you'll explore and become proficient in using these and other libraries to solve real-world problems and develop machine learning models efficiently.

Chapter 2: Data Preprocessing and Exploration

Section 2.1: Data Cleaning and Imputation

Data preprocessing is a critical step in any machine learning project. It involves cleaning and preparing the raw data to make it suitable for analysis and model training. In this section, we will focus on data cleaning and imputation, which are essential processes for handling missing or inconsistent data.

Data Cleaning

Data cleaning is the process of identifying and correcting errors or inconsistencies in a dataset. These errors can be introduced during data collection, entry, or storage and can significantly impact the quality of machine learning models.

Common data cleaning tasks include:

1. **Handling Missing Values:** Identifying and dealing with missing values is a crucial part of data cleaning. Missing values can lead to biased or inaccurate results. Common strategies for handling missing values include removing rows or columns with missing data, filling missing values with a specific value (e.g., mean or median), or using more advanced imputation techniques.

2. **Removing Duplicate Entries:** Duplicate entries can distort analysis and model training. Identifying and removing duplicate rows can help improve the quality of the dataset.

3. **Outlier Detection and Treatment:** Outliers are data points that deviate significantly from the majority of the data. They can affect the accuracy of models. Outlier detection techniques, such as the Z-score or the IQR (Interquartile Range), can be used to identify outliers. Depending on the context, outliers can be removed or transformed.

4. **Standardizing and Normalizing:** Standardizing and normalizing features can ensure that different features have the same scale, making models less sensitive to the scale of input data.

Data Imputation

Data imputation is the process of filling in missing values in a dataset. When dealing with missing data, it's essential to choose an appropriate imputation strategy based on the nature of the data and the problem you are trying to solve.

Common data imputation techniques include:

1. **Mean, Median, or Mode Imputation:** This involves filling missing values with the mean, median, or mode of the respective feature. It is a simple and commonly used method but may not be suitable for all datasets.

```
# Example of mean imputation using Pandas
import pandas as pd

# Fill missing values in the 'Age' column with the mean
df['Age'].fillna(df['Age'].mean(), inplace=True)
```

2. **Forward Fill (ffill) or Backward Fill (bfill):** These methods propagate the last known value forward or backward to fill missing values in a time series or ordered dataset.

```
# Example of forward fill using Pandas
df['Column'].fillna(method='ffill', inplace=True)
```

3. **Interpolation:** Interpolation methods estimate missing values based on the values of adjacent data points. Linear interpolation is a common technique for time series data.

```
# Example of linear interpolation using Pandas
df['Column'].interpolate(method='linear', inplace=True)
```

4. **Machine Learning-Based Imputation:** More advanced imputation methods involve training machine learning models to predict missing values based on other features. Techniques like K-nearest neighbors imputation or regression imputation fall into this category.

```
# Example of K-nearest neighbors imputation using scikit-learn
from sklearn.impute import KNNImputer

imputer = KNNImputer(n_neighbors=2)
df_filled = imputer.fit_transform(df)
```

Data cleaning and imputation are critical steps to ensure that the data you feed into machine learning models is of high quality and doesn't introduce bias or errors. The specific techniques you use will depend on the nature of your dataset and the problem you are trying to solve. By performing these preprocessing steps, you lay a solid foundation for effective machine learning model training and analysis.

Section 2.2: Data Transformation and Scaling

Data transformation and scaling are essential preprocessing steps in machine learning. These techniques help make the data more suitable for modeling and improve the performance of many machine learning algorithms. In this section, we'll explore the concepts of data transformation and scaling and their practical applications.

Data Transformation

Data transformation involves modifying the features or variables in your dataset to make them more informative or to conform to certain assumptions of machine learning algorithms. Some common data transformation techniques include:

1. Log Transformation

The log transformation is used when data exhibits exponential growth or has a long-tailed distribution. It helps make the data more symmetric and reduces the impact of extreme values.

```
# Example of log transformation using NumPy
import numpy as np

# Apply log transformation to a feature 'X'
X_transformed = np.log(X)
```

2. Box-Cox Transformation

The Box-Cox transformation is a family of power transformations that can stabilize variance and make the data more normally distributed. It is particularly useful for improving the performance of linear regression models.

```
# Example of Box-Cox transformation using SciPy
from scipy import stats

# Apply Box-Cox transformation to a feature 'X'
X_transformed, _ = stats.boxcox(X)
```

3. Feature Engineering

Feature engineering involves creating new features from existing ones to capture relevant information better. For example, creating interaction terms, polynomial features, or one-hot encoding categorical variables are common feature engineering techniques.

```
# Example of creating polynomial features using scikit-learn
from sklearn.preprocessing import PolynomialFeatures

poly = PolynomialFeatures(degree=2)
X_poly = poly.fit_transform(X)
```

Data Scaling

Data scaling ensures that all features have the same scale or range. Scaling is crucial for algorithms that are sensitive to the magnitude of features, such as gradient descent-based optimization algorithms and distance-based algorithms. Common data scaling techniques include:

1. Min-Max Scaling (Normalization)

Min-Max scaling scales features to a specific range, typically between 0 and 1. It preserves the relationships between data points but shifts and scales them to fit within the specified range.

```
# Example of Min-Max scaling using scikit-learn
from sklearn.preprocessing import MinMaxScaler

scaler = MinMaxScaler()
X_scaled = scaler.fit_transform(X)
```

2. Standardization (Z-Score Scaling)

Standardization scales features to have a mean of 0 and a standard deviation of 1. It is suitable when the data follows a normal distribution, and it does not bound the features to a specific range.

```
# Example of standardization using scikit-learn
from sklearn.preprocessing import StandardScaler

scaler = StandardScaler()
X_standardized = scaler.fit_transform(X)
```

3. Robust Scaling

Robust scaling is similar to standardization but is less sensitive to outliers. It scales features based on the median and interquartile range (IQR) rather than the mean and standard deviation.

```
# Example of robust scaling using scikit-learn
from sklearn.preprocessing import RobustScaler

scaler = RobustScaler()
X_robust_scaled = scaler.fit_transform(X)
```

When to Apply Data Transformation and Scaling

The decision to apply data transformation and scaling depends on the characteristics of your data and the machine learning algorithms you plan to use. Some algorithms, such as decision trees and random forests, are insensitive to feature scaling and may not require scaling. However, algorithms like support vector machines (SVM), k-nearest neighbors (KNN), and neural networks often benefit from scaled data.

Data transformation techniques should be applied when the data distribution violates the assumptions of a particular model or when it helps improve model performance.

In summary, data transformation and scaling are crucial preprocessing steps in machine learning. These techniques help ensure that your data is in a form that allows machine learning algorithms to perform optimally. By choosing the right transformations and scaling methods, you can enhance the effectiveness of your machine learning models and achieve better results.

Section 2.3: Exploratory Data Analysis (EDA)

Exploratory Data Analysis (EDA) is a critical step in the data preprocessing and analysis pipeline. It involves the systematic exploration and visualization of data to gain insights, identify patterns, and uncover relationships between variables. EDA helps data scientists and analysts understand the characteristics of the dataset, which, in turn, informs feature selection, modeling decisions, and hypothesis testing.

The Goals of EDA

EDA serves several important goals:

1. **Data Understanding:** EDA helps you become familiar with the dataset, including its structure, size, and key attributes. You gain insights into the types of variables present, their data types, and any missing or unusual values.

2. **Pattern Discovery:** EDA allows you to identify patterns, trends, and anomalies within the data. You can visually inspect distributions, correlations, and other statistical properties.

3. **Feature Selection:** EDA assists in selecting relevant features for modeling. By understanding the relationships between features and their importance, you can make informed decisions about which features to include or exclude in your analysis.

4. **Hypothesis Testing:** EDA can help generate hypotheses about the relationships between variables. These hypotheses can be tested rigorously in later stages of the analysis.

Common EDA Techniques

1. **Summary Statistics:** Start by computing summary statistics for numerical features, including measures such as mean, median, standard deviation, and percentiles. For categorical variables, calculate frequencies and proportions.

2. **Data Visualization:** Visualization is a powerful tool for EDA. Create histograms, box plots, scatter plots, and bar charts to visualize the distribution of data, detect outliers, and identify trends. Libraries like Matplotlib and Seaborn in Python are commonly used for this purpose.

```
# Example of creating a histogram using Matplotlib
import matplotlib.pyplot as plt

plt.hist(data['Age'], bins=20)
plt.xlabel('Age')
```

```
plt.ylabel('Frequency')
plt.title('Histogram of Age')
plt.show()
```

3. **Correlation Analysis:** Examine the relationships between numerical variables using correlation matrices or heatmaps. High correlations may indicate potential multicollinearity, which can affect modeling.

```
# Example of correlation heatmap using Seaborn
import seaborn as sns

correlation_matrix = data.corr()
sns.heatmap(correlation_matrix, annot=True, cmap='coolwarm')
plt.title('Correlation Heatmap')
plt.show()
```

4. **Data Distribution:** Explore the distribution of data points and check for normality. Normality tests, like the Shapiro-Wilk test, can help determine if data follows a Gaussian distribution.

5. **Feature Engineering:** Based on EDA insights, perform feature engineering to create new features or transformations of existing ones that may improve model performance.

6. **Handling Outliers:** Identify and handle outliers, which can significantly impact model training. Depending on the context, outliers can be removed, transformed, or kept as-is.

7. **Categorical Variables:** Explore the distribution of categorical variables using bar charts and frequency tables. Consider one-hot encoding or label encoding for categorical variables before modeling.

8. **Time Series Analysis:** For time series data, perform time series-specific EDA, including autocorrelation analysis, trend decomposition, and seasonality detection.

9. **Geospatial Analysis:** If your data contains geographic information, use geospatial visualization techniques to uncover spatial patterns and relationships.

Iterative Process

EDA is often an iterative process, intertwined with data preprocessing and modeling. As you gain insights from initial EDA, you may refine your preprocessing steps, select different features, and adapt your modeling approach accordingly. It's essential to document your findings and insights throughout the EDA process, as they inform the entire data analysis pipeline and contribute to more robust and accurate models.

In conclusion, Exploratory Data Analysis is a fundamental step in understanding and preparing data for machine learning. Through visualizations, summary statistics, and statistical tests, EDA allows data scientists to uncover patterns, relationships, and anomalies within the data, ultimately guiding feature selection and modeling decisions. A well-executed EDA process contributes to the success of data-driven projects by providing a solid foundation for subsequent analysis and modeling steps.

Section 2.4: Feature Engineering

Feature engineering is a crucial aspect of the data preprocessing pipeline in machine learning. It involves creating new features or transforming existing ones to make the data more informative for modeling. Effective feature engineering can significantly impact the performance of machine learning models. In this section, we'll explore the concept of feature engineering and various techniques used in this process.

The Importance of Feature Engineering

Feature engineering is essential for the following reasons:

1. **Improved Model Performance:** Well-engineered features can capture important patterns and relationships in the data, leading to better model performance.

2. **Dimensionality Reduction:** Feature engineering can help reduce the dimensionality of the data by selecting the most relevant features, which can lead to faster training and simpler models.

3. **Handling Non-Linearity:** Sometimes, transforming features can make the data more amenable to linear models, improving their performance.

4. **Dealing with Missing Data:** Feature engineering can involve handling missing values in a way that maximizes the usefulness of the available information.

5. **Domain-Specific Knowledge:** Domain knowledge can be leveraged to create features that capture important aspects of the problem, such as seasonality in time series data or semantic information in text data.

Common Feature Engineering Techniques

1. **Creating Interaction Terms:** Interaction terms are new features created by combining two or more existing features. For example, in a housing price prediction model, multiplying the number of bedrooms by the number of bathrooms can create a new feature that represents the total number of bathroom-bedroom pairs.

2. **Polynomial Features:** Introducing polynomial features can capture non-linear relationships in the data. For example, if a linear model is not sufficient, you can add squared or cubed versions of features.

```python
# Example of creating polynomial features using scikit-learn
from sklearn.preprocessing import PolynomialFeatures

poly = PolynomialFeatures(degree=2)
X_poly = poly.fit_transform(X)
```

3. **Binning or Discretization:** Continuous numerical features can be binned into discrete categories. For example, age can be binned into age groups like "young," "middle-aged," and "elderly."

4. **One-Hot Encoding:** Categorical variables can be one-hot encoded to convert them into a numerical format suitable for many machine learning algorithms.

```
# Example of one-hot encoding using Pandas
encoded_data = pd.get_dummies(data, columns=['Category'])
```

5. **Feature Scaling:** Scaling features to a similar range can help models that are sensitive to feature magnitudes. Common scaling methods include Min-Max scaling and Standardization.

6. **Handling Date and Time:** For time series data, features like day of the week, month, or season can be extracted from date-time variables.

7. **Text Data Processing:** In Natural Language Processing (NLP), text data can be transformed into numerical features using techniques like TF-IDF (Term Frequency-Inverse Document Frequency) or word embeddings (e.g., Word2Vec).

8. **Feature Extraction:** In image analysis, features can be extracted using techniques like Principal Component Analysis (PCA) or convolutional neural networks (CNNs).

The Role of Domain Knowledge

Domain knowledge plays a significant role in feature engineering. Understanding the problem domain and the meaning of features can help identify relevant interactions, transformations, or new feature creation. Experts in the field often provide valuable insights for feature engineering.

Iterative Process

Feature engineering is typically an iterative process that involves experimentation. It's common to try different feature engineering techniques, evaluate their impact on model performance, and refine the features based on the results. It's essential to maintain a balance between feature complexity and model interpretability and to avoid overfitting.

In conclusion, feature engineering is a critical step in data preprocessing for machine learning. It involves creating or transforming features to make them more suitable for modeling and can lead to improved model performance. Effective feature engineering requires a combination of data analysis skills, domain knowledge, and creativity. By carefully engineering features, data scientists can extract valuable information from raw data and build models that generalize well to real-world scenarios.

Section 2.5: Handling Categorical Data

Categorical data is a common type of data that represents discrete categories or labels rather than numerical values. Handling categorical data is a crucial part of data preprocessing in machine learning, as many algorithms require numerical inputs. In this section, we'll explore various techniques for handling categorical data effectively.

Types of Categorical Data

Categorical data can be broadly categorized into two types:

1. **Nominal Data:** Nominal data represents categories with no inherent order or ranking. Examples include colors, types of fruits, or country names.

2. **Ordinal Data:** Ordinal data represents categories with a specific order or ranking. Examples include education levels (e.g., "high school," "bachelor's degree," "master's degree") or customer satisfaction ratings (e.g., "poor," "average," "excellent").

Techniques for Handling Categorical Data

1. One-Hot Encoding

One-hot encoding is a widely used technique for converting categorical variables into a numerical format that can be used by machine learning algorithms. It creates binary columns for each category and assigns a 1 or 0 to indicate the presence or absence of a category.

```python
# Example of one-hot encoding using scikit-learn
from sklearn.preprocessing import OneHotEncoder

encoder = OneHotEncoder()
encoded_data = encoder.fit_transform(data[['Category']]).toarray()
```

2. Label Encoding

Label encoding assigns a unique integer to each category in an ordinal variable. It's suitable for ordinal data where there is a meaningful order among categories.

```python
# Example of label encoding using scikit-learn
from sklearn.preprocessing import LabelEncoder

encoder = LabelEncoder()
data['Education'] = encoder.fit_transform(data['Education'])
```

3. Ordinal Encoding

Ordinal encoding is used for ordinal data and explicitly defines the order of categories. You map each category to a numerical value based on its rank.

```
# Example of ordinal encoding using a dictionary mapping
education_mapping = {'High School': 1, 'Bachelor\'s Degree': 2, 'Master\'s De
gree': 3}
data['Education'] = data['Education'].map(education_mapping)
```

4. Binary Encoding

Binary encoding combines the benefits of one-hot encoding and label encoding. It first assigns a unique integer to each category and then converts the integers to binary code.

5. Frequency Encoding

Frequency encoding replaces categories with their corresponding frequencies in the dataset. This can be useful when the frequency of occurrence of categories is informative.

```
# Example of frequency encoding using Pandas
category_frequencies = data['Category'].value_counts()
data['Category'] = data['Category'].map(category_frequencies)
```

6. Target Encoding

Target encoding (also known as mean encoding) replaces each category with the mean of the target variable (usually the dependent variable) for that category. It can be helpful when the target variable exhibits different behavior across categories.

```
# Example of target encoding using Pandas
category_means = data.groupby('Category')['Target'].mean().to_dict()
data['Category'] = data['Category'].map(category_means)
```

Handling High Cardinality

High cardinality refers to categorical variables with a large number of unique categories. One-hot encoding such variables can lead to a significant increase in the dimensionality of the dataset. To address this, you can:

1. **Top N Categories:** Keep only the top N most frequent categories and group the rest into a new category called "Other."

2. **Frequency or Target Encoding:** Instead of one-hot encoding, use frequency or target encoding to represent high-cardinality variables.

Dealing with Missing Data in Categorical Variables

Handling missing values in categorical variables is essential. You can:

1. **Create a New Category:** Assign a unique category (e.g., "Unknown" or "Missing") to missing values.

2. **Impute with Mode:** Replace missing values with the mode (most frequent category) of the variable.

3. **Predictive Imputation:** Use machine learning models to predict missing values based on other variables.

In conclusion, handling categorical data is a critical part of data preprocessing in machine learning. The choice of encoding method depends on the type of categorical variable and the characteristics of the dataset. Proper handling of categorical data ensures that machine learning algorithms can effectively use this information to make accurate predictions or classifications.

Chapter 3: Supervised Learning: Regression

Section 3.1: Understanding Regression

Regression is a fundamental concept in supervised machine learning, particularly for solving problems where the goal is to predict a continuous numerical outcome. In this section, we'll explore the fundamental principles of regression, its applications, and the types of problems it can address.

What is Regression?

Regression is a type of supervised learning that focuses on predicting a continuous target variable based on one or more input features. The target variable, also known as the dependent variable, is the quantity we want to predict or explain, while the input features, also known as independent variables, are used to make these predictions.

The relationship between the input features and the target variable is modeled mathematically. The regression model attempts to capture and quantify the relationship so that it can be used for making predictions on new, unseen data.

Applications of Regression

Regression analysis is widely used in various fields and domains for solving a wide range of problems, including:

1. **Predictive Modeling:** In finance, regression models can be used to predict stock prices, currency exchange rates, or real estate prices based on historical data and relevant features.

2. **Healthcare:** Regression can help predict patient outcomes, such as disease progression, based on clinical variables and medical history.

3. **Economics:** Economists use regression to model and understand the relationships between economic factors, such as GDP, inflation, and unemployment.

4. **Marketing:** Regression is used for sales forecasting, market analysis, and determining the impact of advertising campaigns on product sales.

5. **Environmental Science:** Regression models can predict environmental factors like temperature, rainfall, or pollution levels based on geographical and climatic features.

Types of Regression

There are several types of regression models, each suited to different types of problems and data:

1. **Linear Regression:** Linear regression is one of the simplest and most commonly used regression techniques. It assumes a linear relationship between the input features and the target variable. The goal is to find the best-fit straight line that minimizes the sum of squared errors.

```python
# Example of linear regression using scikit-learn
from sklearn.linear_model import LinearRegression

# Create a linear regression model
model = LinearRegression()

# Fit the model to the data
model.fit(X, y)

# Make predictions
predictions = model.predict(X_new)
```

2. **Multiple Linear Regression:** Multiple linear regression extends linear regression to multiple input features, allowing for more complex relationships between the features and the target variable.

3. **Polynomial Regression:** Polynomial regression models nonlinear relationships by adding polynomial terms to the linear regression equation.

4. **Ridge and Lasso Regression:** These are regularization techniques that prevent overfitting in linear regression models by adding a penalty term to the loss function.

5. **Support Vector Regression (SVR):** SVR is a regression technique that uses support vector machines to find the best-fit hyperplane.

6. **Decision Tree Regression:** Decision tree regression models the target variable as a piecewise constant function.

7. **Random Forest Regression:** Random forest regression is an ensemble technique that combines multiple decision trees to improve prediction accuracy.

8. **Gradient Boosting Regression:** Gradient boosting builds an additive model by iteratively adding weak learners (usually decision trees) to improve prediction accuracy.

Model Evaluation in Regression

To assess the performance of a regression model, various evaluation metrics are used, including:

1. **Mean Absolute Error (MAE):** MAE measures the average absolute difference between the predicted and actual values. It is less sensitive to outliers.

2. **Mean Squared Error (MSE):** MSE measures the average squared difference between the predicted and actual values. It penalizes large errors more heavily than MAE.

3. **Root Mean Squared Error (RMSE):** RMSE is the square root of MSE and provides a measure of the average magnitude of errors in the same units as the target variable.

4. **R-squared (R2):** R-squared measures the proportion of the variance in the target variable that is explained by the model. It ranges from 0 to 1, with higher values indicating better model fit.

In summary, regression is a fundamental technique in machine learning for predicting continuous numerical outcomes based on input features. It has a wide range of applications and offers various types of models suited to different types of data and relationships. Understanding the principles of regression and how to evaluate regression models is essential for data scientists and analysts working on predictive modeling tasks.

Section 3.2: Simple Linear Regression

Simple Linear Regression is one of the foundational techniques in regression analysis. It models the relationship between a single independent variable (predictor) and a continuous target variable. In this section, we'll delve into the principles of Simple Linear Regression, its mathematical representation, and how to implement it using Python.

The Simple Linear Regression Model

The Simple Linear Regression model assumes that there exists a linear relationship between the independent variable (X) and the target variable (Y). Mathematically, it is represented as:

$$[Y = \_0 + \_1 X +]$$

- (Y) is the target variable.
- (X) is the independent variable.
- (_0) is the intercept (y-intercept) of the linear regression line.
- (_1) is the slope of the linear regression line.
- ( ) represents the error term, which accounts for the variability in (Y) that is not explained by the linear relationship with (X).

The goal in Simple Linear Regression is to estimate the values of (_0) and (_1) such that the linear regression line fits the data points as closely as possible.

Estimating the Coefficients

The coefficients (_0) and (_1) are estimated using the least squares method, which minimizes the sum of squared errors (SSE) between the predicted values and the actual values of the target variable. The formulas for estimating the coefficients are as follows:

$[\_1 =]$

$[\_0 = \{Y\} - \_1\{X\}]$

Where: - (_1) is the estimated slope. - (_0) is the estimated intercept. - (n) is the number of data points. - (X_i) and (Y_i) are the individual data points. - ({X}) and ({Y}) are the means of the independent variable and the target variable, respectively.

Implementing Simple Linear Regression in Python

Let's implement Simple Linear Regression in Python using the scikit-learn library:

```python
# Import the necessary libraries
import numpy as np
import matplotlib.pyplot as plt
from sklearn.linear_model import LinearRegression

# Generate sample data
X = np.array([1, 2, 3, 4, 5])
Y = np.array([2, 3.5, 3.7, 5.5, 6.0])

# Reshape X to a 2D array (required by scikit-learn)
X = X.reshape(-1, 1)

# Create a LinearRegression model
model = LinearRegression()

# Fit the model to the data
model.fit(X, Y)

# Get the estimated coefficients
intercept = model.intercept_
slope = model.coef_[0]

# Make predictions for new data points
new_X = np.array([6, 7, 8]).reshape(-1, 1)
predictions = model.predict(new_X)

# Plot the data points and regression line
plt.scatter(X, Y, label='Data')
plt.plot(X, model.predict(X), color='red', label='Regression Line')
plt.xlabel('X')
plt.ylabel('Y')
plt.legend()
plt.show()
```

In this example, we create a Simple Linear Regression model, fit it to the data, estimate the coefficients, and make predictions for new data points. The result is a regression line that represents the linear relationship between the variables.

To evaluate the performance of a Simple Linear Regression model, we typically use metrics such as Mean Absolute Error (MAE), Mean Squared Error (MSE), and R-squared (R2), as mentioned in Section 3.1. These metrics help assess how well the model fits the data and how accurately it makes predictions.

In summary, Simple Linear Regression is a foundational technique in regression analysis that models the linear relationship between a single independent variable and a continuous target variable. By estimating the coefficients using the least squares method, we can create a linear regression line that represents this relationship. Python libraries like scikit-learn make it easy to implement and evaluate Simple Linear Regression models.

Section 3.3: Multiple Linear Regression

Multiple Linear Regression is an extension of Simple Linear Regression, allowing us to model the relationship between multiple independent variables (predictors) and a continuous target variable. In this section, we'll explore the principles of Multiple Linear Regression, its mathematical representation, and how to implement it using Python.

The Multiple Linear Regression Model

The Multiple Linear Regression model extends the Simple Linear Regression model to include multiple independent variables. Mathematically, it is represented as:

$$[Y = \_0 + \_1 X\_1 + \_2 X\_2 + + \_p X\_p +]$$

- (Y) is the target variable.
- (X_1, X_2, , X_p) are the independent variables.
- (_0) is the intercept (y-intercept) of the regression equation.
- (_1, _2, , _p) are the coefficients of the independent variables.
- ( ) represents the error term, which accounts for the variability in (Y) that is not explained by the linear relationship with the independent variables.

The goal in Multiple Linear Regression is to estimate the values of the coefficients ((_0, _1, , _p)) such that the linear regression equation fits the data points as closely as possible.

Estimating the Coefficients

Similar to Simple Linear Regression, the coefficients ((_0, _1, , _p)) in Multiple Linear Regression are estimated using the least squares method. The formulas for estimating the coefficients are more complex, as they involve matrix operations, but the underlying principle is the same: minimize the sum of squared errors between the predicted values and the actual values of the target variable.

The coefficients are estimated as follows:

$[= (^T)^{-1} ^T]$

Where: - ( ) is the vector of estimated coefficients. - ( ) is the matrix of independent variables (including a column of ones for the intercept). - ( ) is the vector of target variable values.

Implementing Multiple Linear Regression in Python

Let's implement Multiple Linear Regression in Python using the scikit-learn library:

```python
# Import the necessary libraries
import numpy as np
import pandas as pd
from sklearn.linear_model import LinearRegression

# Create sample data
data = pd.DataFrame({'X1': [1, 2, 3, 4, 5], 'X2': [3, 4, 5, 6, 7], 'Y': [2, 3
.5, 3.7, 5.5, 6.0]})

# Separate independent variables (X) and the target variable (Y)
X = data[['X1', 'X2']]
Y = data['Y']

# Create a Multiple Linear Regression model
model = LinearRegression()

# Fit the model to the data
model.fit(X, Y)

# Get the estimated coefficients
intercept = model.intercept_
coefficients = model.coef_

# Make predictions for new data points
new_data = pd.DataFrame({'X1': [6, 7], 'X2': [8, 9]})
predictions = model.predict(new_data)

# Print the estimated coefficients and predictions
print(f'Intercept: {intercept}')
print(f'Coefficients: {coefficients}')
print(f'Predictions: {predictions}')
```

In this example, we create a Multiple Linear Regression model, fit it to the data, estimate the coefficients, and make predictions for new data points. The result is a linear regression equation that models the relationship between the multiple independent variables and the target variable.

Model Evaluation in Multiple Linear Regression

To evaluate the performance of a Multiple Linear Regression model, we can use the same evaluation metrics as in Simple Linear Regression, such as Mean Absolute Error (MAE), Mean Squared Error (MSE), and R-squared (R2). These metrics help assess how well the model fits the data and how accurately it makes predictions.

In summary, Multiple Linear Regression is an extension of Simple Linear Regression that allows us to model the relationship between multiple independent variables and a continuous target variable. By estimating the coefficients using the least squares method, we can create a linear regression equation that represents this relationship. Python libraries like scikit-learn make it easy to implement and evaluate Multiple Linear Regression models for real-world data analysis and prediction tasks.

Section 3.4: Polynomial Regression

Polynomial Regression is a type of regression analysis that extends Simple Linear Regression by modeling the relationship between the independent variable(s) and the target variable as an nth-degree polynomial. In this section, we'll explore the principles of Polynomial Regression, its mathematical representation, and how to implement it using Python.

The Polynomial Regression Model

The Polynomial Regression model assumes that the relationship between the independent variable ((X)) and the target variable ((Y)) can be represented by an nth-degree polynomial equation:

$$[Y = \_0 + \_1 X + \_2 X^2 + \_3 X^3 + + \_n X^n +]$$

- (Y) is the target variable.
- (X) is the independent variable.
- (_0) is the intercept (y-intercept) of the regression equation.
- (_1, _2, , _n) are the coefficients of the polynomial terms.
- () represents the error term, which accounts for the variability in (Y) that is not explained by the polynomial relationship with (X).

The choice of the polynomial degree ((n)) determines the complexity of the model and how well it fits the data. Higher-degree polynomials can capture more complex relationships but may also be prone to overfitting.

Estimating the Coefficients

In Polynomial Regression, the coefficients ((_0, _1, , _n)) are estimated using the least squares method, similar to Linear Regression. However, the polynomial features ((X^2, X^3, , X^n)) are created from the original independent variable ((X)) before fitting the model.

Implementing Polynomial Regression in Python

Let's implement Polynomial Regression in Python using the scikit-learn library:

```python
# Import the necessary libraries
import numpy as np
import matplotlib.pyplot as plt
from sklearn.preprocessing import PolynomialFeatures
from sklearn.linear_model import LinearRegression

# Generate sample data
X = np.array([1, 2, 3, 4, 5])
Y = np.array([2, 3.5, 3.7, 5.5, 6.0])

# Reshape X to a 2D array (required by scikit-learn)
X = X.reshape(-1, 1)

# Define the degree of the polynomial
degree = 2  # Change this value to specify the degree

# Create polynomial features
poly = PolynomialFeatures(degree=degree)
X_poly = poly.fit_transform(X)

# Create a LinearRegression model
model = LinearRegression()

# Fit the model to the polynomial features
model.fit(X_poly, Y)

# Get the estimated coefficients
intercept = model.intercept_
coefficients = model.coef_

# Make predictions for new data points
new_X = np.array([6, 7, 8]).reshape(-1, 1)
new_X_poly = poly.transform(new_X)
predictions = model.predict(new_X_poly)

# Plot the data points and regression curve
plt.scatter(X, Y, label='Data')
plt.plot(X, model.predict(X_poly), color='red', label='Polynomial Regression'
)
plt.xlabel('X')
plt.ylabel('Y')
plt.legend()
plt.show()
```

In this example, we create a Polynomial Regression model of a specified degree, fit it to the polynomial features created from the original data, estimate the coefficients, and make predictions for new data points. The result is a polynomial curve that models the relationship between the independent variable and the target variable.

The evaluation of Polynomial Regression models is similar to that of Linear Regression models. You can use metrics like Mean Absolute Error (MAE), Mean Squared Error (MSE), and R-squared (R2) to assess how well the polynomial curve fits the data and how accurately it makes predictions.

In summary, Polynomial Regression is a flexible regression technique that models the relationship between the independent variable and the target variable as an nth-degree polynomial. It allows us to capture more complex relationships in the data but requires careful consideration of the polynomial degree to avoid overfitting. Python libraries like scikit-learn provide tools for implementing and evaluating Polynomial Regression models for various real-world applications.

Section 3.5: Evaluation Metrics for Regression Models

In the field of regression analysis, it's essential to evaluate the performance of regression models to understand how well they fit the data and make accurate predictions. In this section, we'll explore common evaluation metrics used for regression models, including Mean Absolute Error (MAE), Mean Squared Error (MSE), Root Mean Squared Error (RMSE), and R-squared (R2).

1. Mean Absolute Error (MAE)

Mean Absolute Error (MAE) is a straightforward metric that measures the average absolute difference between the predicted values and the actual values. It quantifies how far, on average, the predictions are from the true values. MAE is calculated as:

$$[= \_{i=1}^{n} |Y\_i - \_i|]$$

Where: - (Y_i) is the actual value of the target variable for the (i)-th data point. - (_i) is the predicted value of the target variable for the (i)-th data point. - (n) is the total number of data points.

2. Mean Squared Error (MSE)

Mean Squared Error (MSE) is another commonly used metric that measures the average of the squared differences between the predicted values and the actual values. It emphasizes larger errors more than MAE, as it squares the differences. MSE is calculated as:

$$[= \_{i=1}^{n} (Y\_i - \_i)^2]$$

MSE is useful for identifying outliers and penalizing models more for large prediction errors.

3. Root Mean Squared Error (RMSE)

Root Mean Squared Error (RMSE) is a modified version of MSE, and it provides a measure of the average magnitude of errors in the same units as the target variable. RMSE is calculated as the square root of MSE:

[=]

RMSE is a popular metric because it is easy to interpret and is sensitive to the scale of the target variable.

4. R-squared (R2)

R-squared (R2) is a metric that measures the proportion of the variance in the target variable that is explained by the regression model. It ranges from 0 to 1, where higher values indicate a better fit of the model to the data. R2 is calculated as:

$[R^2 = 1 -]$

Where: - SSR (Sum of Squared Residuals) is the sum of the squared differences between the predicted values and the mean of the target variable. - SST (Total Sum of Squares) is the sum of the squared differences between the actual values and the mean of the target variable.

R2 = 1 indicates a perfect fit, while R2 = 0 indicates that the model does not explain any variance in the target variable.

Choosing the Right Evaluation Metric

The choice of the evaluation metric depends on the specific problem and the characteristics of the data. Here are some considerations:

- **MAE:** Use MAE when you want a metric that is less sensitive to outliers and provides the absolute magnitude of errors.

- **MSE and RMSE:** Use MSE or RMSE when you want to penalize larger errors more and when the scale of the target variable is meaningful.

- **R2:** Use R2 when you want to understand how well the model explains the variance in the target variable.

It's common to use multiple metrics to evaluate regression models to get a comprehensive understanding of their performance.

In conclusion, evaluation metrics for regression models play a crucial role in assessing the accuracy and effectiveness of these models in predicting continuous target variables. The choice of the metric depends on the specific goals of the analysis and the characteristics of the data. Careful selection and interpretation of these metrics are essential for making informed decisions in regression analysis.

Chapter 4: Supervised Learning: Classification

Section 4.1: Introduction to Classification

Classification is a fundamental concept in supervised machine learning, focusing on the categorization of data into predefined classes or categories based on the input features. In this section, we'll explore the principles of classification, its applications, and the types of problems it can address.

What is Classification?

Classification is a type of supervised learning that deals with predicting the class or category of an object or observation based on its input features. The goal is to build a model that can learn the underlying patterns or decision boundaries in the data to make accurate predictions about the class labels.

In classification tasks, the target variable is categorical, and the model assigns each observation to one of several possible classes. For example, classifying emails as spam or not spam, identifying diseases based on medical test results, or recognizing handwritten digits are all classification problems.

Applications of Classification

Classification is widely used across various domains for solving a wide range of problems, including:

1. **Image Classification:** Identifying objects or patterns within images, such as recognizing animals in photographs.

2. **Text Classification:** Categorizing text data, such as sentiment analysis of customer reviews.

3. **Medical Diagnosis:** Diagnosing diseases or conditions based on patient data and medical test results.

4. **Credit Scoring:** Predicting creditworthiness of individuals for loan approval.

5. **Natural Language Processing (NLP):** Classifying text into categories, such as news articles into topics.

6. **Object Detection:** Identifying and locating objects within images or videos, such as self-driving car applications.

Types of Classification

There are several types of classification algorithms, each suited to different types of data and problem characteristics:

1. **Binary Classification:** In binary classification, there are two possible classes or categories. The model assigns each observation to one of these two classes. Examples include spam detection and disease diagnosis (e.g., presence or absence of a disease).

2. **Multiclass Classification:** Multiclass classification deals with problems where there are more than two possible classes. The model assigns each observation to one of several classes. Examples include handwritten digit recognition (10 classes for digits 0-9) and image recognition (multiple object categories).

3. **Multi-label Classification:** In multi-label classification, each observation can belong to multiple classes simultaneously. This is common in applications like text categorization, where a document can be associated with multiple topics or themes.

Model Evaluation in Classification

Evaluating the performance of a classification model is crucial to assess its accuracy and effectiveness. Common evaluation metrics for classification models include:

1. **Accuracy:** The proportion of correctly classified observations out of the total number of observations. While accuracy is a common metric, it may not be suitable for imbalanced datasets, where one class dominates.

2. **Precision:** The proportion of true positive predictions (correctly predicted positive cases) out of all positive predictions. Precision measures the model's ability to avoid false positives.

3. **Recall (Sensitivity or True Positive Rate):** The proportion of true positive predictions out of all actual positive cases. Recall measures the model's ability to identify all positive cases.

4. **F1 Score:** The harmonic mean of precision and recall. It balances both metrics and is useful when you want to consider both false positives and false negatives.

5. **Confusion Matrix:** A table that shows the true positive, true negative, false positive, and false negative counts, providing insights into the model's performance.

In summary, classification is a key concept in supervised machine learning, used to categorize data into predefined classes based on input features. It has a wide range of applications and offers various types of algorithms suited to different types of data and problem characteristics. Evaluating classification models using appropriate metrics helps in assessing their accuracy and effectiveness in making class predictions.

Section 4.2: Logistic Regression

Logistic Regression is a widely used classification algorithm that models the probability of an observation belonging to a particular class. Despite its name, it is used for classification rather than regression tasks. In this section, we will delve into the principles of Logistic Regression, its mathematical foundation, and its implementation using Python.

Understanding Logistic Regression

Logistic Regression is suitable for binary and multiclass classification problems. It predicts the probability of an observation belonging to a specific class using the logistic function (also known as the sigmoid function). The logistic function maps any real-valued number to a value between 0 and 1, which can be interpreted as a probability.

The logistic function is defined as:

[P(Y=1) =]

- (P(Y=1)) is the probability of the observation belonging to class 1.
- (X_1, X_2, , X_p) are the input features.
- (_0, _1, , _p) are the coefficients to be estimated.

The logistic function produces an S-shaped curve, which is used to model the probability of an event occurring. If the probability is greater than or equal to 0.5, the observation is predicted to belong to class 1; otherwise, it is predicted to belong to class 0.

Estimating Coefficients

The logistic regression model aims to estimate the coefficients ((_0, _1, , _p)) that maximize the likelihood of the observed data. The estimation process is typically done using optimization algorithms like gradient descent.

The logistic regression model does not provide a closed-form solution for the coefficients, as is the case with linear regression. Instead, it uses the logistic function to transform linear combinations of the input features into probabilities.

Implementing Logistic Regression in Python

Let's implement Logistic Regression in Python using the scikit-learn library:

```python
# Import the necessary libraries
import numpy as np
from sklearn.datasets import load_iris
from sklearn.model_selection import train_test_split
from sklearn.linear_model import LogisticRegression
from sklearn.metrics import accuracy_score, classification_report

# Load the Iris dataset (a multiclass classification problem)
data = load_iris()
X = data.data
y = data.target

# Split the dataset into training and testing sets
X_train, X_test, y_train, y_test = train_test_split(X, y, test_size=0.3, rand
```

```
om_state=42)

# Create a Logistic Regression model
model = LogisticRegression(max_iter=1000)

# Fit the model to the training data
model.fit(X_train, y_train)

# Make predictions on the testing data
y_pred = model.predict(X_test)

# Evaluate the model
accuracy = accuracy_score(y_test, y_pred)
report = classification_report(y_test, y_pred)

# Print the accuracy and classification report
print(f'Accuracy: {accuracy}')
print(f'Classification Report:\n{report}')
```

In this example, we load the Iris dataset (a multiclass classification problem), split it into training and testing sets, create a Logistic Regression model, fit it to the training data, make predictions on the testing data, and evaluate the model's accuracy and classification performance.

Model Evaluation in Logistic Regression

Model evaluation in Logistic Regression often involves metrics such as accuracy, precision, recall, F1 score, and the ROC curve. These metrics help assess the model's ability to correctly classify observations into their respective classes and its overall performance.

Logistic Regression is a powerful classification algorithm widely used in various applications, including spam detection, disease diagnosis, and customer churn prediction, among others. Its simplicity and interpretability make it a popular choice for binary and multiclass classification problems.

Section 4.3: Decision Trees and Random Forests

Decision Trees and Random Forests are powerful and interpretable machine learning algorithms commonly used for classification tasks. In this section, we will explore the principles behind Decision Trees and how Random Forests, an ensemble technique, improve their performance.

Decision Trees

A Decision Tree is a hierarchical tree-like structure consisting of nodes that represent decisions or tests on input features. Each node has branches corresponding to different outcomes or classes. Decision Trees are used for both classification and regression tasks, but we will focus on classification in this section.

The Decision Tree algorithm recursively splits the dataset into subsets based on the most significant feature at each node. The splitting process continues until a stopping criterion is met, such as a maximum depth, minimum number of samples in a node, or a purity threshold (e.g., Gini impurity or entropy).

Splitting Criteria

Two common splitting criteria for decision trees in classification are:

- **Gini Impurity:** It measures the probability of misclassifying a randomly chosen element if it were randomly classified according to the distribution of classes in the node.

- **Entropy:** It measures the level of disorder or impurity in a node. Entropy is minimized when all samples in a node belong to a single class.

Random Forests

While Decision Trees are powerful, they can be prone to overfitting, where the model captures noise in the data. Random Forests address this issue by combining multiple Decision Trees into an ensemble model.

Random Forests work as follows:

1. Randomly select a subset of the training data (bootstrapping) to create multiple training datasets.
2. Build a Decision Tree on each dataset independently.
3. During tree construction, consider only a random subset of features at each node.
4. Combine the predictions of all trees through voting (for classification) or averaging (for regression) to make the final prediction.

Random Forests reduce overfitting and improve model generalization by aggregating the predictions of multiple trees. They are robust and suitable for complex datasets with high-dimensional features.

Implementing Decision Trees and Random Forests in Python

Let's implement Decision Trees and Random Forests in Python using the scikit-learn library:

```python
# Import the necessary libraries
import numpy as np
from sklearn.datasets import load_iris
from sklearn.model_selection import train_test_split
from sklearn.tree import DecisionTreeClassifier
from sklearn.ensemble import RandomForestClassifier
from sklearn.metrics import accuracy_score, classification_report
```

```python
# Load the Iris dataset (a multiclass classification problem)
data = load_iris()
X = data.data
y = data.target

# Split the dataset into training and testing sets
X_train, X_test, y_train, y_test = train_test_split(X, y, test_size=0.3, rand
om_state=42)

# Create a Decision Tree model
decision_tree = DecisionTreeClassifier()

# Fit the Decision Tree model to the training data
decision_tree.fit(X_train, y_train)

# Make predictions on the testing data using the Decision Tree
y_pred_tree = decision_tree.predict(X_test)

# Create a Random Forest model
random_forest = RandomForestClassifier(n_estimators=100, random_state=42)

# Fit the Random Forest model to the training data
random_forest.fit(X_train, y_train)

# Make predictions on the testing data using the Random Forest
y_pred_forest = random_forest.predict(X_test)

# Evaluate the Decision Tree and Random Forest models
accuracy_tree = accuracy_score(y_test, y_pred_tree)
report_tree = classification_report(y_test, y_pred_tree)

accuracy_forest = accuracy_score(y_test, y_pred_forest)
report_forest = classification_report(y_test, y_pred_forest)

# Print the accuracy and classification reports for both models
print("Decision Tree:")
print(f'Accuracy: {accuracy_tree}')
print(f'Classification Report:\n{report_tree}')

print("\nRandom Forest:")
print(f'Accuracy: {accuracy_forest}')
print(f'Classification Report:\n{report_forest}')
```

In this example, we load the Iris dataset, split it into training and testing sets, create a Decision Tree model, fit it to the training data, make predictions using the Decision Tree, and then do the same for a Random Forest model. Finally, we evaluate both models using accuracy and classification reports.

Model Evaluation in Decision Trees and Random Forests

Decision Trees and Random Forests can be evaluated using various metrics, including accuracy, precision, recall, F1 score, and the ROC curve. Random Forests often outperform individual Decision Trees in terms of accuracy and generalization, making them a preferred choice for many classification tasks. However, Decision Trees remain valuable for their interpretability and simplicity.

Section 4.4: Support Vector Machines (SVM)

Support Vector Machines (SVMs) are a powerful class of supervised machine learning algorithms used for classification and regression tasks. In this section, we will focus on their application in classification problems.

Understanding Support Vector Machines

SVMs are known for their effectiveness in handling both linear and nonlinear classification tasks. The core idea behind SVMs is to find the optimal hyperplane that maximizes the margin between different classes in the feature space. The "support vectors" are the data points closest to the hyperplane and play a crucial role in defining the margin.

Linear SVM

In linear SVM, the goal is to find the best hyperplane that separates two classes. The hyperplane is represented by the equation:

$[w^T X + b = 0]$

Where: - (w) is the weight vector. - (X) is the input feature vector. - (b) is the bias term.

The decision boundary is given by ($w^T X + b = 0$), and the margin is the distance between this hyperplane and the nearest data points from both classes. SVM aims to maximize this margin.

Nonlinear SVM

In cases where data is not linearly separable, SVM can still be used effectively by transforming the feature space into a higher-dimensional space where separation becomes possible. This transformation is achieved using a kernel function, such as the polynomial kernel or radial basis function (RBF) kernel. The SVM algorithm then finds the optimal hyperplane in the transformed space.

Hyperparameter Tuning

SVMs have important hyperparameters that can significantly affect their performance, such as the choice of the kernel function and the regularization parameter (C). Hyperparameter tuning is crucial for obtaining the best results.

- **(C):** The regularization parameter controls the trade-off between maximizing the margin and minimizing classification errors. Smaller values of (C) result in a wider margin but may allow some misclassifications, while larger values of (C) lead to a narrower margin and fewer misclassifications.

- **Kernel Function:** The choice of the kernel function determines how the data is transformed into a higher-dimensional space. Common kernel functions include the linear kernel, polynomial kernel, and RBF kernel.

Implementing SVM in Python

Let's implement a linear SVM for a binary classification problem using Python's scikit-learn library:

```python
# Import the necessary libraries
import numpy as np
from sklearn.datasets import load_iris
from sklearn.model_selection import train_test_split
from sklearn.svm import SVC
from sklearn.metrics import accuracy_score, classification_report

# Load the Iris dataset (a multiclass classification problem)
data = load_iris()
X = data.data
y = data.target

# Convert the problem into binary classification (class 0 vs. others)
y_binary = np.where(y == 0, 1, 0)

# Split the dataset into training and testing sets
X_train, X_test, y_train, y_test = train_test_split(X, y_binary, test_size=0.
3, random_state=42)

# Create a linear SVM model
svm_model = SVC(kernel='linear', C=1)

# Fit the SVM model to the training data
svm_model.fit(X_train, y_train)

# Make predictions on the testing data
y_pred_svm = svm_model.predict(X_test)

# Evaluate the SVM model
accuracy_svm = accuracy_score(y_test, y_pred_svm)
report_svm = classification_report(y_test, y_pred_svm)

# Print the accuracy and classification report
print("Support Vector Machine:")
```

```
print(f'Accuracy: {accuracy_svm}')
print(f'Classification Report:\n{report_svm}')
```

In this example, we load the Iris dataset, convert it into a binary classification problem (class 0 vs. others), split it into training and testing sets, create a linear SVM model, fit it to the training data, make predictions, and evaluate the model using accuracy and a classification report.

Model Evaluation in SVM

Model evaluation in SVM includes metrics such as accuracy, precision, recall, F1 score, and the ROC curve. SVMs are particularly effective when dealing with high-dimensional data and can handle both linear and nonlinear classification tasks. The choice of the kernel function and hyperparameters should be carefully tuned to achieve the best results for a specific problem.

Section 4.5: Evaluation Metrics for Classification Models

When working with classification models, it's crucial to assess their performance accurately to make informed decisions. In this section, we will explore common evaluation metrics used for classification models. These metrics help us understand how well a model is performing and whether it is suitable for a particular task.

Accuracy

Accuracy is one of the most straightforward metrics for classification. It measures the ratio of correctly predicted instances to the total number of instances in the dataset. While it is easy to understand, accuracy can be misleading, especially in imbalanced datasets. In cases where one class dominates the dataset, a classifier that always predicts the majority class can achieve a high accuracy, even if it's not providing useful predictions for the minority class.

[=]

Precision

Precision measures the ratio of correctly predicted positive instances to the total number of instances predicted as positive. It assesses the classifier's ability to avoid false positives. Precision is particularly important in scenarios where false positives have significant consequences, such as medical diagnoses or fraud detection.

[=]

Recall (Sensitivity or True Positive Rate)

Recall measures the ratio of correctly predicted positive instances to the total number of actual positive instances. It evaluates the classifier's ability to identify all positive cases.

Recall is crucial when missing a positive case can have severe consequences, such as in disease detection.

[=]

F1 Score

The F1 score is the harmonic mean of precision and recall. It balances both metrics and provides a single score that considers both false positives and false negatives. It is especially useful when you want to strike a balance between precision and recall.

[=]

Specificity (True Negative Rate)

Specificity measures the ratio of correctly predicted negative instances to the total number of actual negative instances. It is the complement of recall for the negative class and is essential when correctly identifying negative cases is crucial.

[=]

Receiver Operating Characteristic (ROC) Curve and Area Under the Curve (AUC)

The ROC curve is a graphical representation of a classifier's performance as the discrimination threshold varies. It plots the true positive rate (recall) against the false positive rate for different threshold values. The AUC represents the area under the ROC curve and provides a single score to quantify the classifier's overall performance. AUC values range from 0 to 1, where higher values indicate better performance.

Confusion Matrix

A confusion matrix is a table that summarizes the performance of a classification model. It presents the counts of true positives, true negatives, false positives, and false negatives. The confusion matrix provides insights into the types of errors the model makes and can help in fine-tuning the classifier.

Cross-Validation

Cross-validation is a technique used to assess a model's performance on multiple subsets of the data. It helps detect overfitting and provides a more reliable estimate of a model's generalization performance. Common cross-validation methods include k-fold cross-validation and stratified k-fold cross-validation.

Choosing the Right Metric

The choice of evaluation metric depends on the specific problem and the relative importance of precision, recall, and false positives or false negatives. It's essential to consider the context and consequences of different types of errors when selecting the most suitable metric for a classification task.

In conclusion, evaluation metrics for classification models play a critical role in assessing their performance and suitability for a given task. Each metric provides a different perspective on a model's performance, and the choice of metric should align with the objectives and constraints of the problem at hand.

Chapter 5: Unsupervised Learning: Clustering

Section 5.1: Clustering Concepts

Clustering is a fundamental concept in unsupervised machine learning, focusing on grouping similar data points together based on their inherent patterns or characteristics. In this section, we will explore the principles of clustering, its applications, and common clustering algorithms.

What is Clustering?

Clustering, also known as cluster analysis, is the process of dividing a dataset into groups or clusters in such a way that data points within the same cluster are more similar to each other than to those in other clusters. The goal is to discover hidden patterns, structures, or natural groupings in the data without any prior knowledge of class labels.

Clustering can be useful for various purposes, such as customer segmentation, anomaly detection, image segmentation, and recommendation systems. It helps in identifying subpopulations within a dataset, which can lead to better insights and decision-making.

Key Concepts in Clustering

Distance or Similarity Metric

One of the key aspects of clustering is defining a measure of similarity or dissimilarity between data points. Common metrics include Euclidean distance, Manhattan distance, cosine similarity, and more. The choice of metric depends on the nature of the data and the problem.

Centroids

In centroid-based clustering algorithms, each cluster is represented by a centroid, which is a data point that serves as the center of the cluster. The centroid is often calculated as the mean or median of the data points in the cluster.

Clustering Algorithms

There are various clustering algorithms, each with its own approach to grouping data points. Some of the most popular clustering algorithms include:

- **K-Means Clustering:** Divides the data into a predefined number of clusters (k) by minimizing the sum of squared distances between data points and their cluster centroids.

- **Hierarchical Clustering:** Builds a hierarchy of clusters by iteratively merging or splitting clusters based on a similarity criterion. It results in a dendrogram, which can be cut at different levels to obtain clusters.

- **Density-Based Clustering:** Identifies clusters as dense regions separated by areas of lower point density. DBSCAN (Density-Based Spatial Clustering of Applications with Noise) is a well-known density-based algorithm.

- **Agglomerative Clustering:** A type of hierarchical clustering that starts with individual data points as clusters and merges them step by step until a stopping criterion is met.

- **Spectral Clustering:** Uses spectral graph theory to create a similarity matrix and then applies a dimensionality reduction technique to cluster the data in a lower-dimensional space.

Evaluation of Clustering

Evaluating the quality of clustering results can be challenging because unsupervised learning lacks ground truth labels. However, there are several methods for assessing the quality of clusters, such as silhouette score, Davies-Bouldin index, and visual inspection.

Applications of Clustering

Clustering has a wide range of applications across different domains:

- **Customer Segmentation:** Clustering helps businesses group customers with similar preferences for targeted marketing strategies.

- **Image Segmentation:** In computer vision, clustering is used to segment images into regions with similar characteristics, enabling object detection and analysis.

- **Anomaly Detection:** Clustering can identify unusual patterns or outliers in data, which is valuable for fraud detection and network security.

- **Recommendation Systems:** Grouping users or items with similar behavior or characteristics can enhance recommendation algorithms.

- **Biology and Genetics:** Clustering is applied in gene expression analysis and identifying subgroups of patients based on medical data.

In summary, clustering is a fundamental concept in unsupervised machine learning that involves grouping similar data points together based on their inherent patterns. Clustering algorithms help discover hidden structures in data, and the choice of algorithm and evaluation method depends on the problem at hand. Clustering finds applications in a wide range of fields, making it a valuable tool for data analysis and decision-making.

Section 5.2: K-Means Clustering

K-Means Clustering is one of the most widely used clustering algorithms in unsupervised machine learning. It partitions a dataset into a predetermined number of clusters (k) based on the similarity of data points. In this section, we will delve into the details of the K-Means algorithm, its implementation, and its applications.

How K-Means Clustering Works

The K-Means algorithm follows these steps:

1. **Initialization:** Randomly select k data points from the dataset as initial cluster centroids.

2. **Assignment:** Assign each data point to the nearest cluster centroid based on a distance metric, often using Euclidean distance.

3. **Update Centroids:** Recalculate the centroids of each cluster as the mean of the data points assigned to that cluster.

4. **Repeat:** Repeat the assignment and centroid update steps iteratively until convergence. Convergence typically occurs when the centroids no longer change significantly or when a predefined number of iterations is reached.

Choosing the Number of Clusters (k)

One critical aspect of K-Means is determining the appropriate number of clusters (k) for a given dataset. Selecting an incorrect value for k can lead to suboptimal results. Common methods for choosing k include the elbow method and silhouette score.

- **Elbow Method:** Plot the within-cluster sum of squares (WCSS) for a range of k values and look for an "elbow" point, where the rate of decrease in WCSS slows down. The elbow point indicates a reasonable value for k.

- **Silhouette Score:** Calculate the silhouette score for different values of k. The silhouette score measures the quality of clusters, with higher values indicating better-defined clusters.

K-Means Implementation in Python

Let's implement K-Means clustering in Python using the scikit-learn library:

```python
# Import the necessary libraries
import numpy as np
from sklearn.datasets import make_blobs
from sklearn.cluster import KMeans
import matplotlib.pyplot as plt

# Generate synthetic data for clustering (you can replace this with your data
set)
X, _ = make_blobs(n_samples=300, centers=4, random_state=42)

# Create a K-Means model with a specified number of clusters (k)
kmeans = KMeans(n_clusters=4, random_state=42)
```

```
# Fit the K-Means model to the data
kmeans.fit(X)

# Get cluster assignments for each data point
labels = kmeans.labels_

# Get cluster centroids
centroids = kmeans.cluster_centers_

# Visualize the data points and cluster centroids
plt.scatter(X[:, 0], X[:, 1], c=labels, cmap='viridis')
plt.scatter(centroids[:, 0], centroids[:, 1], marker='x', s=200, linewidths=3
, color='r')
plt.title("K-Means Clustering")
plt.show()
```

In this example, we generate synthetic data using make_blobs, create a K-Means model with a specified number of clusters (k), fit the model to the data, and visualize the clustering results.

Applications of K-Means Clustering

K-Means clustering finds applications in various fields:

- **Image Compression:** Reducing the number of colors in an image by clustering similar pixel colors.

- **Customer Segmentation:** Grouping customers with similar buying behavior for targeted marketing.

- **Document Clustering:** Organizing documents into topics or categories based on their content.

- **Anomaly Detection:** Identifying anomalies or outliers in data by treating normal data points as clusters.

- **Recommender Systems:** Grouping users or items based on behavior for collaborative filtering.

K-Means is versatile and easy to implement, making it a popular choice for various clustering tasks. However, it has limitations, such as sensitivity to the initial placement of centroids and difficulty handling clusters of varying shapes and sizes. In such cases, more advanced clustering algorithms like hierarchical clustering or DBSCAN may be more suitable.

Section 5.3: Hierarchical Clustering

Hierarchical Clustering is a versatile clustering algorithm used to build a hierarchy of clusters in a dataset. It is particularly useful when you want to explore different levels of granularity in clustering results. In this section, we will explore the principles of hierarchical clustering, its variants, and how to implement it.

How Hierarchical Clustering Works

The process of hierarchical clustering can be summarized as follows:

1. **Initialization:** Treat each data point as a single cluster, resulting in as many initial clusters as there are data points.

2. **Merge Clusters:** Repeatedly merge the two closest clusters into a single cluster until only one cluster remains, forming a hierarchical tree-like structure known as a dendrogram.

3. **Dendrogram:** The dendrogram provides a visual representation of the merging process, with data points or clusters at the leaves and the root representing the entire dataset.

Types of Hierarchical Clustering

There are two main types of hierarchical clustering:

Agglomerative Hierarchical Clustering

In agglomerative clustering, also known as "bottom-up" clustering, each data point starts as its own cluster, and clusters are successively merged. The algorithm calculates distances between data points or clusters and merges the closest ones at each step. This process continues until all data points belong to a single cluster.

Divisive Hierarchical Clustering

In divisive clustering, also known as "top-down" clustering, all data points initially belong to a single cluster, and clusters are recursively split into smaller clusters. This process continues until each data point is in its cluster.

Linkage Methods

Hierarchical clustering requires a method for measuring the distance or similarity between clusters. Common linkage methods include:

- **Single Linkage:** The distance between two clusters is defined as the shortest distance between any pair of data points in the two clusters. It tends to produce long, thin clusters.

- **Complete Linkage:** The distance between two clusters is defined as the maximum distance between any pair of data points in the two clusters. It tends to produce compact, spherical clusters.

- **Average Linkage:** The distance between two clusters is defined as the average distance between all pairs of data points in the two clusters. It balances between single and complete linkage.

- **Ward's Linkage:** Minimizes the variance within each cluster when merging clusters. It often results in well-balanced and compact clusters.

Dendrogram Cutting

To obtain a specific number of clusters from the dendrogram, you can "cut" it at a certain height or distance level. The choice of the cut-off point determines the number of clusters and should align with the problem's requirements.

Hierarchical Clustering Implementation in Python

Let's implement agglomerative hierarchical clustering in Python using the scikit-learn library:

```python
# Import the necessary libraries
import numpy as np
import matplotlib.pyplot as plt
from sklearn.datasets import make_blobs
from sklearn.cluster import AgglomerativeClustering
from scipy.cluster.hierarchy import dendrogram, linkage

# Generate synthetic data for clustering (you can replace this with your data
set)
X, _ = make_blobs(n_samples=300, centers=4, random_state=42)

# Create an Agglomerative Clustering model with a specified number of cluster
s
agg_clustering = AgglomerativeClustering(n_clusters=4)

# Fit the model to the data
agg_clustering.fit(X)

# Plot the dendrogram
linked = linkage(X, method='ward')
dendrogram(linked, orientation='top', distance_sort='descending', show_leaf_c
ounts=True)
plt.title("Hierarchical Clustering Dendrogram")
plt.xlabel("Data Points")
plt.ylabel("Distance")
plt.show()
```

In this example, we generate synthetic data, create an Agglomerative Clustering model, fit it to the data, and visualize the dendrogram using scipy's dendrogram function.

Hierarchical clustering is used in various domains:

- **Biology:** Classifying species based on genetic data or grouping genes with similar expression patterns.

- **Image Analysis:** Segmenting images into regions with similar properties.

- **Document Clustering:** Organizing documents into topics or categories based on their content.

- **Social Network Analysis:** Identifying communities or groups of users with similar behavior.

- **Market Segmentation:** Grouping customers with similar purchasing behavior for targeted marketing.

Hierarchical clustering offers flexibility in exploring different levels of granularity in clustering results, making it valuable for understanding complex datasets. However, it may not be suitable for very large datasets due to its computational complexity.

Section 5.4: Density-Based Clustering

Density-Based Clustering is a clustering technique that focuses on identifying dense regions of data points separated by areas of lower point density. Unlike K-Means and Hierarchical Clustering, which require a predefined number of clusters, density-based methods can discover clusters of varying shapes and sizes. In this section, we will explore Density-Based Spatial Clustering of Applications with Noise (DBSCAN), one of the most popular density-based clustering algorithms.

How DBSCAN Works

DBSCAN operates by defining two main parameters:

1. **Epsilon (ε):** A radius that specifies the maximum distance between two data points for one to be considered as in the neighborhood of the other.

2. **Minimum Points (MinPts):** The minimum number of data points required to form a dense region. A point is considered a core point if there are at least MinPts points within ε distance from it.

The algorithm proceeds as follows:

1. Randomly select an unvisited data point.

2. If the point is a core point (has at least MinPts points within ε distance), create a new cluster and add the core point and all reachable points within ε distance to the cluster.

3. Repeat steps 1 and 2 until no more core points can be found.

4. If there are unvisited points, select another unvisited point and continue the process to create additional clusters.

5. Continue until all data points have been processed.

DBSCAN Implementation in Python

Let's implement DBSCAN clustering in Python using the scikit-learn library:

```python
# Import the necessary libraries
import numpy as np
import matplotlib.pyplot as plt
from sklearn.datasets import make_moons
from sklearn.cluster import DBSCAN

# Generate synthetic data for clustering (you can replace this with your data
set)
X, _ = make_moons(n_samples=200, noise=0.05, random_state=42)

# Create a DBSCAN model with specified parameters (ε and MinPts)
dbscan = DBSCAN(eps=0.3, min_samples=5)

# Fit the model to the data
dbscan.fit(X)

# Get cluster labels (-1 for noise points)
labels = dbscan.labels_

# Visualize the clustering results
plt.scatter(X[:, 0], X[:, 1], c=labels, cmap='viridis')
plt.title("DBSCAN Clustering")
plt.show()
```

In this example, we generate synthetic data using make_moons, create a DBSCAN model with specified ε and MinPts parameters, fit the model to the data, and visualize the clustering results.

Advantages and Limitations of DBSCAN

Advantages of DBSCAN: - Can discover clusters of arbitrary shapes. - Robust to noise and outliers, as it classifies data points outside dense regions as noise. - Does not require specifying the number of clusters in advance.

Limitations of DBSCAN: - Sensitivity to the ε and MinPts parameters, which can affect results. - Struggles with clusters of varying densities. - May not perform well on high-dimensional data due to the curse of dimensionality.

DBSCAN is used in various applications:

- **Spatial Data Analysis:** Identifying spatial clusters of events, such as disease outbreaks.
- **Anomaly Detection:** Detecting unusual patterns or outliers in data.
- **Image Segmentation:** Segmenting images into regions with similar characteristics.
- **Recommendation Systems:** Grouping users with similar preferences.
- **Natural Language Processing:** Clustering text documents based on content similarity.

DBSCAN's ability to handle noise and discover clusters of arbitrary shapes makes it valuable in situations where other clustering methods may struggle. However, careful parameter tuning is essential for obtaining meaningful results.

Section 5.5: Evaluating Clustering Performance

Evaluating the performance of clustering algorithms is essential to ensure the quality of the obtained clusters. Unlike supervised learning, clustering is an unsupervised task, making it challenging to assess clustering results objectively. In this section, we will discuss various methods and metrics used to evaluate clustering performance.

Internal Evaluation Metrics

Internal evaluation metrics assess the quality of clustering without relying on external labels. Some commonly used internal metrics include:

Silhouette Score

The silhouette score measures how similar each data point is to its own cluster compared to other clusters. It ranges from -1 (a poor clustering) to +1 (a perfect clustering), with 0 indicating overlapping clusters.

```python
from sklearn.metrics import silhouette_score

# Calculate the silhouette score for clustering results
silhouette_avg = silhouette_score(X, labels)
```

Davies-Bouldin Index

The Davies-Bouldin index measures the average similarity between each cluster and the cluster that is most similar to it. A lower index value indicates better clustering.

```
from sklearn.metrics import davies_bouldin_score

# Calculate the Davies-Bouldin index for clustering results
db_index = davies_bouldin_score(X, labels)
```

Calinski-Harabasz Index (Variance Ratio Criterion)

The Calinski-Harabasz index measures the ratio of between-cluster variance to within-cluster variance. Higher values indicate better separation between clusters.

```
from sklearn.metrics import calinski_harabasz_score

# Calculate the Calinski-Harabasz index for clustering results
ch_index = calinski_harabasz_score(X, labels)
```

External Evaluation Metrics

External evaluation metrics compare clustering results to external ground-truth labels, when available. Commonly used external metrics include:

Adjusted Rand Index (ARI)

ARI measures the similarity between true labels and predicted clusters, accounting for chance. It ranges from -1 (random clustering) to +1 (perfect clustering).

```
from sklearn.metrics import adjusted_rand_score

# Calculate the Adjusted Rand Index for clustering results
ari = adjusted_rand_score(true_labels, predicted_labels)
```

Normalized Mutual Information (NMI)

NMI measures the mutual information between true labels and predicted clusters, normalized to a value between 0 (no mutual information) and 1 (perfect clustering).

```
from sklearn.metrics import normalized_mutual_info_score

# Calculate the Normalized Mutual Information for clustering results
nmi = normalized_mutual_info_score(true_labels, predicted_labels)
```

Visual Evaluation

Visualization is an essential tool for evaluating clustering results. You can visualize the clusters using scatter plots, heatmaps, or dendrograms (in hierarchical clustering) to gain insights into the quality and structure of the clusters.

Limitations of Evaluation Metrics

It's important to note that no single metric can fully capture the quality of clustering results, and different metrics may lead to different interpretations. Choosing the appropriate evaluation metric depends on the characteristics of the data and the goals of the clustering task.

Selecting the right evaluation metric depends on whether ground-truth labels are available and the specific goals of the clustering task. Internal metrics are suitable when ground-truth labels are not available, while external metrics are useful when evaluating against known labels.

In practice, it's advisable to use a combination of evaluation metrics and visual inspection to assess clustering performance thoroughly. Additionally, parameter tuning and trying different clustering algorithms may be necessary to achieve the desired clustering quality.

Chapter 5: Unsupervised Learning: Clustering 5.1 Clustering Concepts 5.2 K-Means Clustering 5.3 Hierarchical Clustering 5.4 Density-Based Clustering 5.5 Evaluating Clustering Performance

Chapter 6: Dimensionality Reduction

Section 6.1: Why Dimensionality Reduction?

Dimensionality reduction is a fundamental technique in machine learning and data analysis. It involves reducing the number of features (dimensions) in a dataset while preserving the essential information. But why is dimensionality reduction necessary, and what are the motivations behind it? In this section, we'll explore the reasons for employing dimensionality reduction techniques.

1. Curse of Dimensionality

As the number of features (dimensions) in a dataset increases, the data becomes increasingly sparse in the high-dimensional space. This phenomenon, known as the "curse of dimensionality," can lead to several issues, including increased computational complexity, difficulty in visualizing data, and degraded performance of machine learning models. Dimensionality reduction helps alleviate this problem by reducing the number of features.

2. Improved Model Performance

In many cases, high-dimensional data can lead to overfitting. When there are more features than data points, machine learning models can capture noise instead of meaningful patterns. Dimensionality reduction can mitigate overfitting by reducing the number of features and improving the generalization capability of models.

3. Enhanced Visualization

Human intuition and understanding are limited to three dimensions. Visualizing data in high-dimensional spaces is challenging, if not impossible. Dimensionality reduction techniques project data onto a lower-dimensional space, allowing for better visualization and insight into the structure of the data.

4. Faster Training and Inference

Reducing the dimensionality of a dataset often leads to faster training and inference times for machine learning models. This is especially important in real-time or resource-constrained applications where efficiency is a priority.

5. Noise Reduction

High-dimensional data is more likely to contain noise and irrelevant features. By reducing dimensionality, dimensionality reduction methods can filter out noise and focus on the most informative features, improving the quality of the data.

6. Feature Engineering

Dimensionality reduction can be seen as a form of automated feature engineering. It identifies combinations of features that capture the most significant variance in the data, potentially revealing hidden patterns or relationships.

7. Interpretability

Reducing dimensionality can make models and results more interpretable. Instead of dealing with a large number of features, you work with a smaller set of dimensions that may correspond to meaningful concepts or variables.

8. Data Compression

In some applications, reducing dimensionality can lead to data compression, making it more efficient to store and transmit large datasets.

9. Preprocessing for Downstream Tasks

Dimensionality reduction can be used as a preprocessing step for various downstream tasks, such as clustering, classification, and regression. By reducing dimensionality before applying other algorithms, you can often achieve better results.

In summary, dimensionality reduction is a crucial technique for simplifying and improving the analysis of high-dimensional data. It offers numerous benefits, including mitigating the curse of dimensionality, improving model performance, enabling better visualization, and enhancing the overall efficiency of machine learning pipelines. In the following sections, we will delve into specific dimensionality reduction methods and their applications.

Section 6.2: Principal Component Analysis (PCA)

Principal Component Analysis (PCA) is one of the most widely used dimensionality reduction techniques in machine learning and data analysis. It seeks to reduce the dimensionality of a dataset while preserving as much of the variance in the data as possible. PCA accomplishes this by transforming the original features into a new set of linearly uncorrelated variables called principal components.

Key Concepts

1. Principal Components

Principal components are linear combinations of the original features that capture the maximum variance in the data. The first principal component (PC1) explains the most variance, followed by PC2, PC3, and so on. The goal is to retain a subset of these principal components while discarding the rest.

2. Variance Explained

PCA quantifies the amount of variance explained by each principal component. This information is crucial for determining how many principal components to retain. A common practice is to set a threshold for the total explained variance (e.g., 95%) and retain enough principal components to meet or exceed that threshold.

3. Orthogonality

Principal components are orthogonal to each other, meaning they are uncorrelated. This orthogonality property simplifies the interpretation of the new feature space.

4. Dimension Reduction

PCA reduces the dimensionality of the data by projecting it onto a lower-dimensional subspace defined by the selected principal components. The reduced dataset retains the essential information while discarding the less important features.

PCA Implementation in Python

Here's a basic implementation of PCA using the scikit-learn library:

```python
# Import necessary libraries
from sklearn.decomposition import PCA
from sklearn.preprocessing import StandardScaler

# Standardize the data (important for PCA)
scaler = StandardScaler()
X_scaled = scaler.fit_transform(X)

# Create a PCA model with the desired number of components
pca = PCA(n_components=2)  # You can choose the number of components here

# Fit PCA to the scaled data
pca.fit(X_scaled)

# Transform the data to the lower-dimensional space
X_pca = pca.transform(X_scaled)
```

In this example, we first standardize the data to ensure that all features have the same scale. Then, we create a PCA model with the desired number of components (in this case, 2). After fitting the model to the scaled data, we transform the data into the lower-dimensional space defined by the selected principal components.

Applications of PCA

PCA has numerous applications, including:

- **Data Visualization:** Reducing high-dimensional data to two or three principal components for visualization and exploration.

- **Noise Reduction:** Removing noise and irrelevant features from data.

- **Compression:** Reducing the size of datasets while retaining essential information.

- **Feature Engineering:** Creating new features that capture the most significant variation in the data.

- **Preprocessing:** As a preprocessing step for machine learning algorithms to improve model performance.

Limitations of PCA

While PCA is a powerful technique, it has some limitations:

- **Linearity:** PCA assumes linear relationships between features. It may not perform well when data exhibits complex nonlinear relationships.

- **Loss of Interpretability:** The principal components themselves may not have meaningful interpretations in terms of the original features.

- **Loss of Information:** Depending on the number of retained components, some information from the original data may be lost.

- **Data Scaling:** PCA is sensitive to the scale of the features, so data standardization is often necessary.

In summary, PCA is a valuable dimensionality reduction technique that is widely used for simplifying high-dimensional data. It helps with visualization, noise reduction, and feature engineering. However, it is essential to understand its assumptions and limitations when applying PCA to real-world data analysis tasks.

Section 6.3: t-Distributed Stochastic Neighbor Embedding (t-SNE)

t-Distributed Stochastic Neighbor Embedding (t-SNE) is a dimensionality reduction technique primarily used for visualizing high-dimensional data in a lower-dimensional space. Unlike linear techniques like PCA, t-SNE focuses on preserving the pairwise similarities between data points in the original and lower-dimensional spaces. It is particularly useful for visualizing complex, nonlinear structures in data.

Key Concepts

1. Similarity Measurement

t-SNE starts by computing pairwise similarities between data points in the high-dimensional space. These similarities are typically based on a Gaussian distribution centered at each data point, creating a probability distribution of pairwise similarities.

2. Lower-Dimensional Mapping

The goal of t-SNE is to find a lower-dimensional mapping (usually 2D or 3D) in which pairwise similarities are preserved as much as possible. It achieves this by defining a similar probability distribution in the lower-dimensional space.

3. Cost Function

t-SNE minimizes the divergence between the two probability distributions, effectively pulling similar data points closer together in the lower-dimensional space and pushing dissimilar data points apart. This is achieved through an optimization process that minimizes a cost function known as the Kullback-Leibler (KL) divergence.

t-SNE Implementation in Python

Here's a basic implementation of t-SNE using the scikit-learn library:

```python
# Import necessary libraries
from sklearn.manifold import TSNE
from sklearn.preprocessing import StandardScaler

# Standardize the data (important for t-SNE)
scaler = StandardScaler()
X_scaled = scaler.fit_transform(X)

# Create a t-SNE model with the desired number of components and perplexity
tsne = TSNE(n_components=2, perplexity=30)  # You can adjust perplexity as ne
eded

# Fit t-SNE to the scaled data
X_tsne = tsne.fit_transform(X_scaled)
```

In this example, we first standardize the data to ensure that all features have the same scale. Then, we create a t-SNE model with the desired number of components (typically 2 or 3) and a parameter called "perplexity." Perplexity controls the balance between preserving local and global structure in the data. You can adjust it based on your specific visualization needs.

After fitting the t-SNE model to the scaled data, we obtain the lower-dimensional representation of the data in the X_tsne variable.

Applications of t-SNE

t-SNE is primarily used for data visualization, especially when dealing with complex, nonlinear data structures. Some common applications include:

- **Visualizing High-Dimensional Data:** t-SNE is widely used to visualize high-dimensional data in 2D or 3D, making it easier to understand the data's underlying structure.

- **Clustering Validation:** It can be used to validate the quality of clustering results by visualizing how well data points of the same cluster group together in the lower-dimensional space.

- **Feature Engineering:** t-SNE can be used to create new features that capture the essential information in high-dimensional data.

Limitations of t-SNE

While t-SNE is a powerful visualization tool, it has some limitations:

- **Random Initialization:** t-SNE is sensitive to the random initialization of data points, which means that different runs can yield slightly different results.

- **Computationally Intensive:** It can be computationally intensive for large datasets.

- **Interpretability:** The resulting lower-dimensional space may not have a direct interpretation in terms of the original features.

- **Not Suitable for Dimension Reduction:** Unlike PCA, t-SNE is not typically used for dimensionality reduction but for visualization.

In conclusion, t-SNE is a valuable technique for visualizing complex, high-dimensional data by preserving pairwise similarities. It is particularly useful for data exploration, clustering validation, and gaining insights into the structure of data. However, it should be used primarily as a visualization tool rather than for dimensionality reduction.

Section 6.4: Linear Discriminant Analysis (LDA)

Linear Discriminant Analysis (LDA) is a dimensionality reduction technique that focuses on finding the linear combinations of features that best separate different classes or groups within a dataset. LDA is often used in supervised learning settings, where the class labels of data points are known and used to guide the dimensionality reduction process.

Key Concepts

1. Discriminative Power

The primary goal of LDA is to maximize the separability of different classes in the lower-dimensional space. It does this by finding linear projections (discriminants) of the data that maximize the between-class variance while minimizing the within-class variance.

2. Dimensionality Reduction

LDA reduces the dimensionality of the data by projecting it onto a lower-dimensional subspace. In classification tasks, this lower-dimensional space is chosen such that it retains the most discriminatory information between classes.

3. Linear Transformation

The transformation applied by LDA is linear, meaning that it's a weighted sum of the original features. Each component of the linear transformation is a discriminant, and these discriminants are selected to maximize class separation.

4. Assumptions

LDA assumes that the data follows a multivariate normal distribution within each class and that the covariance matrices of different classes are equal. These assumptions make LDA particularly well-suited for classification tasks.

LDA Implementation in Python

Here's a basic implementation of LDA using the scikit-learn library:

```python
# Import necessary libraries
from sklearn.discriminant_analysis import LinearDiscriminantAnalysis
from sklearn.preprocessing import StandardScaler

# Standardize the data (important for LDA)
scaler = StandardScaler()
X_scaled = scaler.fit_transform(X)

# Create an LDA model with the desired number of components
lda = LinearDiscriminantAnalysis(n_components=2)  # You can choose the number
of components here

# Fit LDA to the scaled data
X_lda = lda.fit_transform(X_scaled, y)  # 'y' represents the class labels
```

In this example, we first standardize the data to ensure that all features have the same scale. Then, we create an LDA model with the desired number of components (typically 2) and fit it to the scaled data, along with the corresponding class labels.

Applications of LDA

LDA has several applications, including:

- **Classification:** LDA can be used as a preprocessing step to improve the performance of classification algorithms by reducing dimensionality and enhancing class separability.

- **Feature Engineering:** LDA can be employed to create new features that capture the most discriminative information for classification tasks.

- **Data Visualization:** Similar to PCA and t-SNE, LDA can be used for data visualization, especially in cases where class separation is essential.

- **Reducing Overfitting:** LDA can help reduce overfitting in high-dimensional datasets by removing less informative features.

Limitations of LDA

While LDA is a powerful technique, it has some limitations:

- **Assumptions:** LDA assumes that data follows a multivariate normal distribution within each class and that the covariance matrices of different classes are equal. These assumptions may not hold in all cases.

- **Supervised Nature:** LDA is a supervised technique, meaning it requires class labels for dimensionality reduction. It may not be suitable for unsupervised or semi-supervised tasks.

- **Linearity:** LDA assumes linear relationships between features and classes, which may not be appropriate for all datasets.

In summary, Linear Discriminant Analysis (LDA) is a dimensionality reduction technique that aims to enhance class separability by finding linear combinations of features. It is particularly valuable in supervised classification tasks and can be used for feature engineering and data visualization. However, it is essential to be aware of its assumptions and limitations when applying LDA to real-world data analysis.

Section 6.5: Applications of Dimensionality Reduction

Dimensionality reduction techniques like Principal Component Analysis (PCA), t-Distributed Stochastic Neighbor Embedding (t-SNE), and Linear Discriminant Analysis (LDA) have a wide range of applications across various domains in machine learning and data analysis. In this section, we'll explore some common applications and scenarios where dimensionality reduction plays a crucial role.

Data Visualization

One of the most prominent applications of dimensionality reduction is data visualization. High-dimensional data is challenging to visualize directly, but by reducing its dimensionality to 2D or 3D using techniques like PCA or t-SNE, it becomes easier to create meaningful visualizations. These visualizations help analysts and data scientists gain insights into the structure and patterns within the data.

Here's an example of using PCA for data visualization:

```python
import matplotlib.pyplot as plt
from sklearn.decomposition import PCA

# Apply PCA to reduce data dimensionality
pca = PCA(n_components=2)
X_pca = pca.fit_transform(X)

# Visualize the reduced data
plt.scatter(X_pca[:, 0], X_pca[:, 1], c=y, cmap='viridis')
```

```
plt.xlabel('Principal Component 1')
plt.ylabel('Principal Component 2')
plt.title('PCA Visualization')
plt.show()
```

Noise Reduction

In many real-world datasets, noise and irrelevant features can hinder the performance of machine learning models. Dimensionality reduction can help mitigate this issue by eliminating noisy dimensions. By retaining only the most informative components, the model can focus on the essential aspects of the data, resulting in better generalization.

Feature Engineering

Dimensionality reduction techniques like LDA are used for feature engineering. LDA aims to find linear combinations of features that maximize the separation between different classes. These derived features can be highly effective for classification tasks. Feature engineering using LDA can enhance the performance of machine learning algorithms, especially in scenarios with limited labeled data.

Preprocessing for Machine Learning

Dimensionality reduction is often used as a preprocessing step before applying machine learning algorithms. Reducing the dimensionality of the data can lead to faster model training and improved model performance. It can also help prevent overfitting, especially when dealing with high-dimensional datasets.

Anomaly Detection

Dimensionality reduction can be useful for anomaly detection. By projecting data into a lower-dimensional space, anomalies or outliers may become more apparent. This can aid in identifying data points that deviate significantly from the norm.

Computational Efficiency

In large-scale machine learning tasks, the computational cost of training models on high-dimensional data can be prohibitive. Dimensionality reduction can significantly reduce the computational complexity while preserving essential information. This is particularly beneficial in scenarios where real-time or near-real-time predictions are required.

Limitations and Considerations

While dimensionality reduction techniques offer numerous benefits, it's crucial to consider their limitations and potential drawbacks. Some common considerations include:

- Loss of Information: Dimensionality reduction inherently involves a loss of information. Depending on the chosen number of components, some details from the original data may be discarded.

- Algorithm Selection: The choice of dimensionality reduction algorithm should be made based on the characteristics of the data and the specific goals of the analysis.

- Assumptions: Some techniques, like LDA, make assumptions about data distribution and class separability. It's essential to assess whether these assumptions hold for your data.

- Interpretability: Reduced-dimensional representations may not be as interpretable as the original features, which can be a concern in certain applications.

In conclusion, dimensionality reduction techniques are powerful tools in machine learning and data analysis. They find applications in data visualization, noise reduction, feature engineering, preprocessing, anomaly detection, and computational efficiency improvement. However, their successful application requires careful consideration of the specific task, data, and goals, as well as an understanding of their limitations.

Chapter 7: Model Selection and Hyperparameter Tuning

Section 7.1: Cross-Validation Techniques

In machine learning, model selection and hyperparameter tuning are critical steps in building robust and high-performing models. These processes involve finding the best combination of model algorithms and hyperparameters to optimize a model's performance on unseen data. However, to achieve this, it's essential to avoid overfitting and ensure that the model's performance estimates are reliable. This is where cross-validation techniques come into play.

The Need for Cross-Validation

In typical machine learning workflows, data is divided into a training set and a test set. The training set is used to train the model, while the test set is used to evaluate its performance. However, this approach has limitations:

1. **Data Split Variability:** The choice of which data points go into the training set and which go into the test set can affect the model's performance. A different random split may yield different results.

2. **Limited Data:** In cases where the dataset is small, setting aside a portion for testing can result in insufficient data for training, leading to poor model performance.

3. **Overfitting Risk:** Repeatedly evaluating the model on the same test set can lead to overfitting, where the model learns to perform well specifically on the test data but fails to generalize to new, unseen data.

Cross-Validation Overview

Cross-validation (CV) techniques address these issues by dividing the data into multiple subsets, performing multiple training and testing iterations, and aggregating the results. This provides a more robust estimate of the model's performance and helps avoid overfitting. Here are some common cross-validation techniques:

1. K-Fold Cross-Validation:
- The data is divided into 'K' equally sized folds.
- The model is trained and tested 'K' times, with each fold serving as the test set once.
- The results are averaged to obtain the final performance estimate.

```
from sklearn.model_selection import cross_val_score, KFold
kf = KFold(n_splits=5)   # 5-fold cross-validation
scores = cross_val_score(model, X, y, cv=kf)
```

2. Stratified K-Fold Cross-Validation:
- Similar to K-Fold, but it ensures that each fold has approximately the same class distribution as the entire dataset, especially useful for imbalanced datasets.

```
from sklearn.model_selection import StratifiedKFold
skf = StratifiedKFold(n_splits=5)  # Stratified 5-fold cross-validation
scores = cross_val_score(model, X, y, cv=skf)
```

3. Leave-One-Out Cross-Validation (LOOCV):

- Each data point serves as a test set once, and the rest of the data is used for training.
- Suitable for small datasets but can be computationally expensive for larger ones.

```
from sklearn.model_selection import LeaveOneOut
loo = LeaveOneOut()
scores = cross_val_score(model, X, y, cv=loo)
```

Benefits of Cross-Validation

- **Reliable Performance Estimates:** Cross-validation provides more reliable estimates of a model's performance because it evaluates the model on multiple test sets.

- **Better Generalization:** It helps prevent overfitting by ensuring that the model generalizes well to unseen data.

- **Data Efficiency:** It makes better use of limited data by repeatedly partitioning it into training and test sets.

- **Hyperparameter Tuning:** Cross-validation can be combined with hyperparameter tuning to select the best hyperparameters for a model.

Choosing the Right Cross-Validation Technique

The choice of cross-validation technique depends on factors such as dataset size, class distribution, and computational resources. K-Fold cross-validation is a good starting point for most cases, but stratified K-Fold and LOOCV are useful when dealing with specific challenges.

In conclusion, cross-validation techniques are essential for model selection and hyperparameter tuning in machine learning. They provide more robust performance estimates, improve generalization, and help prevent overfitting, ultimately leading to better-performing models. Choosing the appropriate cross-validation method depends on the characteristics of the dataset and the specific requirements of the task.

Section 7.2: Grid Search and Random Search

In the process of building machine learning models, finding the best combination of hyperparameters is often crucial for achieving optimal performance. Hyperparameters are settings that are not learned from the data but are set before the training process. Examples include the learning rate in a neural network or the depth of a decision tree.

Grid search and random search are two common techniques used for hyperparameter tuning. They help automate the process of systematically exploring different hyperparameter values to find the best configuration for a model.

Grid Search

Grid search is a hyperparameter tuning technique where you specify a grid of hyperparameter values to search over. For each combination of hyperparameters in the grid, the model is trained and evaluated using cross-validation. The combination that results in the best performance is selected as the optimal set of hyperparameters.

Here's a high-level overview of how grid search works:

1. Define a set of hyperparameters and the range of values to search over. For example, you might specify different values for learning rates, the number of trees in a random forest, or regularization strengths.

2. Create a grid of all possible combinations of these hyperparameter values.

3. For each combination in the grid:

   - Train the model with the specified hyperparameters on the training data.
   - Evaluate the model's performance using cross-validation.

4. Select the combination of hyperparameters that yielded the best performance.

Here's an example of grid search using scikit-learn:

```python
from sklearn.model_selection import GridSearchCV
from sklearn.svm import SVC

# Define a grid of hyperparameters to search over
param_grid = {
    'C': [0.1, 1, 10],
    'kernel': ['linear', 'rbf', 'poly'],
    'gamma': [0.1, 1, 'scale']
}

# Create the grid search object
grid_search = GridSearchCV(SVC(), param_grid, cv=5)

# Fit the grid search to the data
grid_search.fit(X_train, y_train)

# Get the best hyperparameters
best_params = grid_search.best_params_
```

Random Search

Random search, as the name suggests, randomly samples hyperparameter values from predefined ranges. This approach is less exhaustive than grid search but can be more efficient in finding good hyperparameter combinations, especially when the search space is vast.

Here's how random search works:

1. Define a distribution or range for each hyperparameter you want to tune. For example, you might specify uniform or log-uniform distributions for continuous hyperparameters.

2. Randomly sample hyperparameter values from these distributions a specified number of times.

3. Train and evaluate a model for each set of sampled hyperparameters using cross-validation.

4. Select the hyperparameters that result in the best performance.

Random search is particularly useful when you have limited computational resources or when you're unsure about which hyperparameters are likely to perform well.

Here's an example of random search using scikit-learn:

```python
from sklearn.model_selection import RandomizedSearchCV
from scipy.stats import uniform

# Define hyperparameter distributions to sample from
param_dist = {
    'C': uniform(0.1, 10),
    'kernel': ['linear', 'rbf', 'poly'],
    'gamma': ['scale', 'auto'] + list(np.logspace(-3, 3, 100))
}

# Create the random search object
random_search = RandomizedSearchCV(SVC(), param_dist, n_iter=100, cv=5)

# Fit the random search to the data
random_search.fit(X_train, y_train)

# Get the best hyperparameters
best_params = random_search.best_params_
```

Grid Search vs. Random Search

The choice between grid search and random search depends on factors like the size of the hyperparameter search space, available computational resources, and time constraints. Grid search is more exhaustive but can be computationally expensive for large search spaces. Random search is a more efficient alternative, especially when you have limited resources or when you're unsure about the hyperparameter distribution.

In conclusion, grid search and random search are valuable tools for hyperparameter tuning in machine learning. They help automate the process of finding the best hyperparameter configurations and can significantly improve the performance of your models. The choice between the two methods should be based on the specific requirements of your problem and the available resources.

Section 7.3: Hyperparameter Tuning Best Practices

Hyperparameter tuning is a crucial step in building machine learning models that perform well on real-world tasks. While grid search and random search provide automated ways to explore hyperparameter configurations, there are several best practices to keep in mind to make the process more efficient and effective.

1. Start with a Coarse Search:

- Begin with a broad search space to quickly identify promising hyperparameter ranges. This helps avoid fine-tuning too early, which can be time-consuming.
- Once you have a sense of the promising regions, narrow down the search space for a finer-grained exploration.

2. Use Prior Knowledge:

- Leverage domain knowledge and insights into your specific problem to inform your choice of hyperparameter values.
- For example, if you know that a learning rate of 0.1 is typically effective for similar tasks, start your search in that range.

3. Use Validation Data:

- Always use a separate validation dataset during hyperparameter tuning to estimate model performance accurately.
- Avoid using the test set for tuning, as it can lead to overfitting to the test data.

4. Implement Early Stopping:

- Incorporate early stopping criteria during training to prevent unnecessary computation. For instance, stop training if the validation performance plateaus.

5. Logarithmic Scales for Parameters:

- When exploring hyperparameters with a wide range of values (e.g., learning rates, regularization strengths), consider using a logarithmic scale.
- This allows you to cover a broad range efficiently without missing important values.

6. Ensemble of Models:

- Create an ensemble of models with different hyperparameters to improve robustness. This technique, known as model stacking or blending, combines predictions from multiple models to make final predictions.

7. Random Search After Grid Search:

- If a grid search initially identifies promising regions, follow it with a random search in those regions. Random search can be more efficient at fine-tuning within specific ranges.

8. Use Specialized Libraries:

- Explore specialized libraries like Optuna, Hyperopt, or Ray Tune, which provide more advanced techniques for hyperparameter optimization.

9. Consider Bayesian Optimization:

- Bayesian optimization methods, such as Gaussian Processes or Tree-structured Parzen Estimators (TPE), can be highly efficient for hyperparameter tuning.

10. Parallelize the Search:

- If you have access to multiple CPUs or GPUs, parallelize the hyperparameter search to speed up the process.

11. Track and Visualize Results:

- Keep a record of hyperparameter configurations and their corresponding perf ormance metrics.
- Visualization tools can help you identify trends and make informed decision s.

12. Regularize Models:

- Use regularization techniques like L1 or L2 regularization to reduce sensit ivity to hyperparameter choices.

13. Evaluate on a Held-Out Test Set:

- After hyperparameter tuning, evaluate the final model on a completely held-out test set to get a realistic estimate of its performance.

14. Iterate as Necessary:

- Hyperparameter tuning is an iterative process. Don't hesitate to revisit an d refine hyperparameters as you gain more insights into your problem.

15. Documentation:

- Document the hyperparameters, configurations, and results thoroughly to ens ure reproducibility.

Remember that hyperparameter tuning is not a one-size-fits-all process. The best practices mentioned above should be adapted to your specific problem, dataset, and available resources. It's also essential to strike a balance between the time spent on tuning and the potential improvements in model performance, as hyperparameter tuning can be computationally expensive.

Section 7.4: Model Evaluation and Selection

After performing hyperparameter tuning using techniques like grid search or random search, it's crucial to evaluate and select the best-performing model. Model evaluation is a critical step in the machine learning pipeline because it helps you choose the model configuration that is most likely to perform well on unseen data. In this section, we'll discuss various aspects of model evaluation and selection.

1. Performance Metrics:
- Start by choosing appropriate performance metrics that align with your problem. For classification tasks, common metrics include accuracy, precision, recall, F1-score, and ROC AUC. For regression, metrics like mean squared error (MSE), mean absolute error (MAE), and R-squared are commonly used.

2. Cross-Validation:
- Use cross-validation to estimate the model's performance more robustly. Techniques like k-fold cross-validation provide a better understanding of how the model generalizes to different subsets of the data.

3. Hold-Out Validation Set:
- Set aside a validation set (different from the test set) to evaluate models during hyperparameter tuning. This helps prevent overfitting to the test set and provides a more realistic estimate of model performance.

4. Model Comparison:
- Compare the performance of different models using your chosen evaluation metrics. Visualizations like ROC curves and precision-recall curves can help you make informed decisions.

5. Overfitting and Underfitting:
- Keep an eye out for signs of overfitting (excellent performance on the training data but poor on validation/test data) or underfitting (poor performance on both training and validation/test data). Adjust hyperparameters accordingly.

6. Bias-Variance Tradeoff:
- Understand the bias-variance tradeoff when selecting models. High-bias models are more likely to underfit, while high-variance models are prone to overfitting.

7. Ensemble Methods:
- Consider ensemble methods like bagging (e.g., Random Forests) and boosting (e.g., AdaBoost, Gradient Boosting) to combine the strengths of multiple models and improve overall performance.

8. Interpretability:

- Depending on your application, consider the interpretability of the model. Simpler models like linear regression or decision trees may be preferred when interpretability is crucial.

9. Regularization:

- Experiment with different levels of regularization to combat overfitting. Techniques like L1 and L2 regularization can be adjusted to control model complexity.

10. Final Test Set:
- After selecting the best model based on cross-validation or validation perf ormance, evaluate it on a separate, held-out test set. This step provides an unbiased estimate of the model's generalization performance.

11. Model Robustness:
- Assess how robust your selected model is to variations in the data, includi ng noise or missing values.

12. Business Objectives:
- Keep in mind the ultimate business or research objectives. The best model m ay vary depending on whether you prioritize precision, recall, or another met ric aligned with your goals.

13. Iterative Process:
- Model evaluation and selection can be an iterative process. Don't hesitate to revisit hyperparameter tuning or try different algorithms if initial resul ts are unsatisfactory.

14. Documentation:
- Document the selected model's configuration, hyperparameters, and evaluatio n results thoroughly. This documentation is essential for reproducibility and future reference.

Remember that the choice of the best model should not solely rely on a single performance metric. It should consider the specific requirements of your problem and the trade-offs between different metrics. Additionally, the choice of the best model may evolve as new data becomes available or as the problem itself evolves. Model evaluation is an ongoing process in machine learning, and continuous monitoring is essential for maintaining model performance over time.

Section 7.5: Avoiding Overfitting and Underfitting

Overfitting and underfitting are common challenges in machine learning that can significantly impact the performance of your models. In this section, we'll explore these issues and discuss strategies to mitigate them.

Overfitting:

Overfitting occurs when a model learns to perform exceptionally well on the training data but fails to generalize to unseen data. Signs of overfitting include a large gap between training and validation/test performance. Here are strategies to combat overfitting:

1. **Regularization:** Use regularization techniques like L1 and L2 regularization to penalize overly complex models. These techniques discourage the model from fitting noise in the data.

2. **Reduce Model Complexity:** Simplify the model architecture by reducing the number of layers, nodes, or features. This can make the model less prone to overfitting.

3. **Increase Data:** Gather more training data if possible. More data can help the model learn patterns more effectively and reduce the likelihood of overfitting.

4. **Data Augmentation:** In computer vision tasks, data augmentation techniques like rotation, flipping, and cropping can artificially increase the size of the training dataset, making the model more robust.

5. **Dropout:** Implement dropout layers in neural networks. Dropout randomly deactivates a fraction of neurons during training, preventing the network from relying too heavily on specific neurons.

6. **Early Stopping:** Use early stopping during training. Monitor the model's performance on a validation set and stop training when performance starts to degrade, indicating overfitting.

7. **Cross-Validation:** Perform k-fold cross-validation to ensure that the model's performance is consistent across different subsets of the data. If performance varies widely, it may be a sign of overfitting.

Underfitting:

Underfitting occurs when a model is too simplistic to capture the underlying patterns in the data. Signs of underfitting include poor performance on both the training and validation/test datasets. Strategies to address underfitting include:

1. **Increase Model Complexity:** If your model is too simple, consider increasing its complexity. This may involve adding more layers, nodes, or features.

2. **Feature Engineering:** Engineer informative features that capture relevant information from the data. Feature selection and transformation can also help improve model performance.

3. **Hyperparameter Tuning:** Adjust hyperparameters like learning rates, regularization strengths, and batch sizes to find a configuration that fits the data better.

4. **Ensemble Methods:** Combine multiple models using ensemble methods like Random Forests or Gradient Boosting. Ensemble methods are robust against underfitting.

5. **Check Data Quality:** Ensure that your training data is clean and representative of the problem. Noisy or biased data can lead to underfitting.

6. **Feature Scaling:** Normalize or standardize features to have similar scales. This can help some models perform better.

7. **Try Different Algorithms:** Experiment with different algorithms to find one that is better suited to your problem. Some algorithms may inherently handle underfitting better than others.

8. **Collect More Data:** In some cases, underfitting may be due to a lack of sufficient training data. Gathering more data can help the model learn better.

9. **Resample Data:** If the dataset is imbalanced, consider resampling techniques like oversampling the minority class or undersampling the majority class to balance the classes.

10. **Iterate and Experiment:** Overcoming underfitting often requires experimentation. Iterate on model architectures and hyperparameters until you achieve a better fit.

Both overfitting and underfitting can be challenging to diagnose, and finding the right balance between model complexity and simplicity is a key part of building effective machine learning models. Regular model evaluation and validation are crucial in identifying and addressing these issues throughout the model development process.

Chapter 8: Ensemble Learning

Ensemble learning is a powerful technique in machine learning that involves combining multiple models to improve predictive performance and reduce overfitting. Instead of relying on a single model, ensemble methods leverage the diversity of multiple models to make more accurate predictions. In this chapter, we will explore the concept of ensemble learning, various ensemble techniques, and how to implement them in practice.

Section 8.1: Ensemble Methods Overview

Ensemble methods are based on the idea that multiple weak learners (models with modest predictive capabilities) can be combined to create a strong learner that outperforms individual models. The key principle behind ensemble learning is "wisdom of the crowd," where the collective decision of multiple models is often more accurate than the decision of any individual model.

Here are some key concepts and terminology related to ensemble methods:

1. **Base Learners:** These are the individual models or algorithms that form the ensemble. They can be of the same type (homogeneous ensemble) or different types (heterogeneous ensemble).

2. **Ensemble Size:** The number of base learners in the ensemble can vary, and it is an important hyperparameter to consider.

3. **Aggregation:** Ensemble methods combine the predictions of base learners using aggregation techniques. The most common aggregation methods are averaging (for regression) and voting (for classification).

4. **Diversity:** The effectiveness of an ensemble often depends on the diversity of its base learners. Diversity can be achieved by training base learners on different subsets of the data or by using different algorithms.

5. **Ensemble Types:** There are several types of ensemble methods, including bagging, boosting, stacking, and more. Each type has its own characteristics and advantages.

Let's briefly introduce some popular ensemble techniques that we will explore in more detail in the subsequent sections:

- **Bagging (Bootstrap Aggregating):** Bagging involves training multiple base learners independently on random subsets of the training data. The final prediction is obtained by averaging (for regression) or voting (for classification) the predictions of individual models. Random Forests are a well-known example of a bagging ensemble.

- **Boosting:** Boosting sequentially trains base learners, where each subsequent learner focuses on the samples that were misclassified by the previous ones. AdaBoost and Gradient Boosting are common boosting algorithms.

- **Stacking:** Stacking combines the predictions of multiple base learners by training a meta-model (also known as a blender) on top of the base learners' outputs. The meta-model learns to make a final prediction based on the predictions of the base learners.

- **Voting:** In ensemble classification, voting methods include majority voting (simple majority rule), weighted voting (assigning different weights to base learners), and soft voting (weighted probabilities). These methods help make decisions based on the consensus of base learners.

Ensemble methods are widely used in practice and have led to significant improvements in predictive modeling across various domains. They are particularly useful when dealing with complex problems or datasets with noisy or incomplete information. In the following sections, we will dive deeper into each of these ensemble techniques and explore how to implement them in Python using popular libraries like scikit-learn.

Section 8.2: Bagging: Bootstrap Aggregating

Bagging, short for Bootstrap Aggregating, is a popular ensemble learning technique that aims to improve the accuracy and robustness of machine learning models. It works by training multiple base learners independently on different subsets of the training data and then aggregating their predictions. Bagging is particularly effective when the base learners are prone to overfitting or when dealing with high-variance models.

How Bagging Works:

1. **Bootstrap Sampling:** Bagging starts by creating multiple random subsets (with replacement) of the training data. Each subset is called a bootstrap sample. Since the sampling is done with replacement, some data points may appear multiple times in a bootstrap sample, while others may not appear at all. This randomness introduces diversity into the training process.

2. **Independent Training:** For each bootstrap sample, a base learner (e.g., decision tree, neural network, etc.) is trained independently. Each base learner learns to capture different patterns in the data due to the variability introduced by the bootstrap samples.

3. **Aggregation:** After training all base learners, bagging combines their predictions to make a final prediction. The aggregation process depends on the type of problem:

   – For regression problems, the predictions are typically averaged.
   – For classification problems, a majority vote is often used to determine the final class label.

Benefits of Bagging:

Bagging offers several benefits:

1. **Reduced Variance:** By training on multiple bootstrap samples, bagging reduces the variance of the model. This helps to make the model more robust and less sensitive to noise in the data.

2. **Improved Generalization:** Bagging often leads to better generalization, as the ensemble can capture a broader range of patterns in the data.

3. **Reduced Overfitting:** It mitigates the risk of overfitting, especially when using complex models that are prone to memorizing the training data.

4. **Parallelizable:** The base learners can be trained in parallel, making bagging suitable for distributed computing.

5. **Model Diversity:** Since base learners are trained independently, they may use different features or learn different aspects of the data, enhancing the ensemble's diversity.

Example Implementation in Python:

Let's illustrate bagging with a simple example using scikit-learn:

```python
from sklearn.ensemble import BaggingClassifier
from sklearn.tree import DecisionTreeClassifier

# Create a base classifier (e.g., decision tree)
base_classifier = DecisionTreeClassifier()

# Create a BaggingClassifier with 100 base classifiers
bagging_classifier = BaggingClassifier(base_classifier, n_estimators=100)

# Fit the ensemble on your training data
bagging_classifier.fit(X_train, y_train)

# Make predictions on new data
predictions = bagging_classifier.predict(X_test)
```

In this example, we create a BaggingClassifier with 100 decision tree base classifiers. The ensemble is then trained on the training data and used to make predictions on new data. The predictions from all base classifiers are aggregated to make the final prediction.

Bagging is a versatile ensemble technique and can be applied to various base learners, making it a valuable tool for improving model performance in a wide range of machine learning tasks.

Section 8.3: Boosting: AdaBoost and Gradient Boosting

Boosting is another powerful ensemble technique in machine learning that focuses on improving the accuracy of models sequentially. Unlike bagging, where base learners are trained independently, boosting trains base learners sequentially, and each new learner corrects the errors made by the previous ones. In this section, we'll explore two popular boosting algorithms: AdaBoost (Adaptive Boosting) and Gradient Boosting.

AdaBoost (Adaptive Boosting):

AdaBoost is one of the earliest and simplest boosting algorithms. It works as follows:

1. **Weighted Data:** Initially, all training samples are assigned equal weights.

2. **Base Learners:** AdaBoost starts by training a base learner (e.g., decision tree) on the weighted training data. It focuses on learning the samples that were misclassified by the previous base learner.

3. **Weight Update:** After each base learner is trained, the weights of misclassified samples are increased, making them more important for the next learner. This

adaptive weight adjustment process continues for a predefined number of iterations or until a performance threshold is reached.

4. **Final Model:** The final prediction is obtained by combining the predictions of all base learners. The base learners that perform well have more influence on the final prediction.

AdaBoost is effective when the base learners are weak learners, meaning they perform slightly better than random chance. AdaBoost gives more weight to difficult-to-classify examples, making it particularly useful in binary classification problems.

Gradient Boosting:

Gradient Boosting is a more sophisticated boosting technique that builds an ensemble by iteratively adding base learners. Unlike AdaBoost, Gradient Boosting uses gradient descent to minimize a loss function, such as mean squared error (for regression) or deviance (for classification). Here's how it works:

1. **Initial Model:** The first base learner is trained on the data.

2. **Residuals:** For subsequent iterations, Gradient Boosting focuses on the errors (residuals) made by the ensemble up to that point. It trains a new base learner to predict these residuals.

3. **Shrinkage:** The predictions of each new base learner are shrunk (multiplied by a learning rate) before being added to the ensemble. This helps prevent overfitting and allows for a more stable convergence.

4. **Stopping Criterion:** The boosting process continues for a predefined number of iterations or until a stopping criterion is met, such as achieving a specified level of performance.

5. **Final Model:** The final prediction is obtained by summing the predictions of all base learners.

Gradient Boosting is known for its high predictive accuracy and is commonly used in both regression and classification tasks. Popular implementations include Gradient Boosting Machines (GBM) and XGBoost.

Example Implementation in Python:

Let's illustrate AdaBoost and Gradient Boosting with scikit-learn:

```python
from sklearn.ensemble import AdaBoostClassifier, GradientBoostingClassifier

# Create AdaBoost and Gradient Boosting classifiers
ada_classifier = AdaBoostClassifier(n_estimators=50)
gbm_classifier = GradientBoostingClassifier(n_estimators=100)

# Fit the classifiers on your training data
```

```
ada_classifier.fit(X_train, y_train)
gbm_classifier.fit(X_train, y_train)

# Make predictions on new data
ada_predictions = ada_classifier.predict(X_test)
gbm_predictions = gbm_classifier.predict(X_test)
```

In this example, we create AdaBoost and Gradient Boosting classifiers, fit them on the training data, and make predictions on new data. These algorithms adaptively learn from the errors of previous iterations to improve their overall accuracy.

Section 8.4: Stacking and Blending

Stacking and blending are advanced ensemble techniques that combine the predictions of multiple machine learning models to improve overall performance. These techniques take a meta-level approach where one or more meta-learners are trained to make predictions based on the outputs of base learners. In this section, we'll explore stacking and blending and discuss their benefits and implementation.

Stacking:

Stacking, also known as stacked generalization, involves the following steps:

1. **Base Learners:** You start by training multiple diverse base learners (e.g., decision trees, support vector machines, neural networks) on the training data.

2. **Hold-Out Data:** A portion of the training data is set aside as a hold-out dataset. The base learners are trained on the remaining data.

3. **First-Level Predictions:** Each base learner makes predictions on the hold-out dataset. These predictions serve as the input features for the meta-learner.

4. **Meta-Learner:** A meta-learner, often a simple model like logistic regression or linear regression, is trained on the first-level predictions. The meta-learner learns to combine the base learners' predictions to make the final prediction.

5. **Final Prediction:** To make predictions on new data, the base learners first make predictions, which are then fed into the trained meta-learner to obtain the final prediction.

Stacking leverages the diversity of base learners to improve model performance, especially when the base learners have different strengths and weaknesses. It can capture complex relationships between base learners' predictions and the target variable.

Blending:

Blending is a simplified version of stacking:

1. **Base Learners:** Like stacking, you train multiple base learners on the training data.

2. **Hold-Out Data:** A portion of the training data is set aside as a hold-out dataset.

3. **First-Level Predictions:** Each base learner makes predictions on the hold-out dataset.

4. **Meta-Learner (Hold-Out):** Unlike stacking, blending doesn't involve a separate meta-learner trained on first-level predictions. Instead, you combine the predictions of base learners on the hold-out dataset using simple averaging or voting.

5. **Final Prediction:** To make predictions on new data, the base learners first make predictions, and their predictions are averaged or voted on for the final prediction.

Blending is a less complex approach compared to stacking and can be a good choice when you want a performance boost without introducing too much complexity.

Benefits and Considerations:

- **Performance Boost:** Both stacking and blending can significantly improve predictive performance by combining the strengths of diverse base learners.

- **Flexibility:** You can choose different types of base learners and meta-learners to suit your specific problem.

- **Complexity:** Stacking is more complex than blending as it involves training a separate meta-learner. Blending is simpler but may offer slightly less performance gain.

- **Data Leakage:** Care should be taken to prevent data leakage when combining predictions from different models. Ensure that the hold-out dataset is not used during base learner training.

Example Implementation in Python:

Here's a simplified example of blending in Python:

```python
from sklearn.model_selection import train_test_split
from sklearn.ensemble import RandomForestClassifier, GradientBoostingClassifi
er
from sklearn.metrics import accuracy_score

# Split the data into training and hold-out sets
X_train, X_holdout, y_train, y_holdout = train_test_split(X, y, test_size=0.2
, random_state=42)

# Create base classifiers
rf_classifier = RandomForestClassifier()
gb_classifier = GradientBoostingClassifier()

# Train base classifiers on the training data
```

```
rf_classifier.fit(X_train, y_train)
gb_classifier.fit(X_train, y_train)

# Make predictions on the hold-out dataset
rf_predictions = rf_classifier.predict(X_holdout)
gb_predictions = gb_classifier.predict(X_holdout)

# Blend predictions using simple averaging
blended_predictions = (rf_predictions + gb_predictions) / 2

# Calculate accuracy of the blended predictions
accuracy = accuracy_score(y_holdout, blended_predictions)
```

In this example, we create two base classifiers (RandomForestClassifier and GradientBoostingClassifier), train them on the training data, and blend their predictions on the hold-out dataset using simple averaging. The accuracy of the blended predictions is calculated to assess performance.

Section 8.5: Building Robust Models with Ensembles

Ensemble methods, including bagging, boosting, stacking, and blending, are powerful techniques for improving the performance and robustness of machine learning models. In this section, we'll discuss the importance of building robust models and how ensembles contribute to achieving this goal.

Robustness in Machine Learning:

Robustness in machine learning refers to a model's ability to perform well across different datasets, especially in the presence of noise, outliers, or variations in the data. Building robust models is crucial for real-world applications where data may be imperfect or subject to changes.

Ensemble methods enhance model robustness in several ways:

1. **Reducing Overfitting:** Ensembles can help reduce overfitting by combining the predictions of multiple base models. When each base model overfits differently, the ensemble's combined prediction tends to be more balanced and less prone to overfitting.

2. **Handling Noisy Data:** Noisy data points or outliers can have a significant impact on model performance. Ensembles are less sensitive to outliers since they consider the collective wisdom of base learners.

3. **Dealing with Variations:** Real-world data can exhibit variations in distribution over time or across different sources. Ensembles adapt to these variations by combining diverse models trained on different subsets of data.

4. **Increased Generalization:** Ensembles often achieve better generalization by leveraging the diversity of base learners. When base learners are trained on different subsets or with different algorithms, they capture different aspects of the underlying data distribution.

Ensemble Strategies for Robustness:

1. **Diverse Base Learners:** To build robust ensembles, it's essential to choose diverse base learners that make different assumptions about the data. Diversity ensures that errors made by one base learner are corrected by others.

2. **Cross-Validation:** Cross-validation techniques, such as k-fold cross-validation, help assess a model's performance on different subsets of data. Ensembles can benefit from cross-validation to ensure their robustness.

3. **Outlier Detection:** Identifying and handling outliers is critical for robustness. You can combine ensembles with outlier detection methods to improve model resilience.

4. **Data Preprocessing:** Proper data preprocessing techniques, such as data cleaning, feature scaling, and dimensionality reduction, contribute to robust model training. Ensembles can be applied to data after preprocessing.

5. **Monitoring and Maintenance:** In production, monitoring the performance of ensemble models is essential for detecting changes in data distribution or other issues. Regular model maintenance and retraining can ensure continued robustness.

Example Implementation in Python:

Here's a simple Python code snippet to illustrate building a robust ensemble using the BaggingClassifier from scikit-learn:

```python
from sklearn.ensemble import BaggingClassifier
from sklearn.tree import DecisionTreeClassifier
from sklearn.model_selection import cross_val_score

# Create a base decision tree classifier
base_classifier = DecisionTreeClassifier()

# Create a BaggingClassifier ensemble with 10 base classifiers
ensemble_classifier = BaggingClassifier(base_classifier, n_estimators=10)

# Evaluate the ensemble's robustness using cross-validation
cross_val_scores = cross_val_score(ensemble_classifier, X, y, cv=5)

# Calculate the mean cross-validation score
mean_score = cross_val_scores.mean()
```

In this example, we create a BaggingClassifier ensemble with 10 base decision tree classifiers and evaluate its robustness using cross-validation. Cross-validation helps assess the model's performance on different subsets of the dataset, contributing to its robustness.

Chapter 9: Neural Networks and Deep Learning

Section 9.1: Introduction to Neural Networks

Neural networks, often referred to as artificial neural networks (ANNs), are a class of machine learning models inspired by the structure and function of the human brain. They have gained immense popularity in recent years due to their ability to tackle complex problems across various domains, including image and speech recognition, natural language processing, and game playing. In this section, we'll provide an introduction to neural networks, covering their basic concepts and components.

Key Concepts:

1. Neurons (Nodes):

At the core of a neural network are artificial neurons, also known as nodes or perceptrons. These nodes are inspired by the biological neurons in the human brain. Each neuron receives input, processes it, and produces an output. Neurons are organized into layers: an input layer, one or more hidden layers, and an output layer.

2. Weights and Connections:

The connections between neurons are represented by weights. Each connection has a weight associated with it, which determines the strength of the connection. During training, these weights are adjusted to optimize the network's performance.

3. Activation Function:

The activation function of a neuron defines how it processes its input and produces an output. Common activation functions include the sigmoid function, ReLU (Rectified Linear Unit), and tanh (hyperbolic tangent). Activation functions introduce non-linearity to the network, allowing it to capture complex relationships in data.

4. Feedforward Propagation:

In a neural network, information flows in a forward direction, from the input layer through the hidden layers to the output layer. This process is known as feedforward propagation. Each neuron's output is computed based on its inputs, weights, and activation function.

5. Backpropagation:

Training a neural network involves adjusting the weights of connections to minimize the difference between the predicted output and the actual target values. Backpropagation is the process of calculating the gradients of the error with respect to the weights and using these gradients to update the weights in the network. This iterative process is performed using optimization algorithms like gradient descent.

Deep learning refers to neural networks with multiple hidden layers, often called deep neural networks. Deep learning has been particularly successful in handling complex and high-dimensional data, leading to breakthroughs in computer vision, natural language understanding, and more.

Types of Neural Networks:

Neural networks come in various architectures, each designed for specific tasks:

- **Feedforward Neural Networks (FNNs):** These networks have information flowing in one direction, from input to output. They are suitable for tasks like classification and regression.

- **Convolutional Neural Networks (CNNs):** CNNs are specialized for processing grid-like data, such as images. They use convolutional layers to automatically learn features from the data.

- **Recurrent Neural Networks (RNNs):** RNNs are designed for sequential data, like time series or natural language. They have connections that allow information to flow in loops, enabling them to capture temporal dependencies.

- **Long Short-Term Memory (LSTM) and Gated Recurrent Unit (GRU):** These are variants of RNNs with improved ability to capture long-range dependencies in sequences.

- **Autoencoders:** Autoencoders are used for unsupervised learning and feature extraction. They consist of an encoder and a decoder, with the goal of learning a compact representation of the input data.

Neural networks have revolutionized machine learning and are a fundamental building block of modern deep learning systems. In the following sections, we will delve deeper into the components and applications of neural networks, including how to build and train them using popular deep learning frameworks like TensorFlow and PyTorch.

Section 9.2: Building a Neural Network in Python

In this section, we'll explore how to build a neural network in Python using popular deep learning libraries such as TensorFlow and Keras. We'll walk through the essential steps involved in creating a neural network for a typical machine learning task. Before we begin, make sure you have TensorFlow and Keras installed. You can install them using pip:

```
pip install tensorflow keras
```

Importing Libraries:

To get started, import the necessary libraries:

```
import tensorflow as tf
from tensorflow import keras
```

Building the Neural Network:

1. **Define the Architecture:** The first step in building a neural network is to define its architecture. You specify the number of layers, the number of neurons in each layer, and the activation functions. Here's an example of a simple feedforward neural network with one hidden layer:

```
model = keras.Sequential([
    keras.layers.Input(shape=(input_shape,)),    # Input layer
    keras.layers.Dense(64, activation='relu'),    # Hidden layer with 64 neuron
s and ReLU activation
    keras.layers.Dense(output_shape, activation='softmax')    # Output layer wi
th softmax activation
])
```

2. **Compile the Model:** After defining the architecture, compile the model. During compilation, you specify the loss function, optimization algorithm, and evaluation metrics. For classification tasks, you often use categorical cross-entropy as the loss function and the Adam optimizer:

```
model.compile(optimizer='adam',
              loss='categorical_crossentropy',
              metrics=['accuracy'])
```

3. **Model Summary:** You can print a summary of the model's architecture to see the number of parameters and layer details:

```
model.summary()
```

4. **Training the Model:** To train the model, provide the training data and labels and specify the number of epochs (iterations over the entire training dataset):

```
model.fit(X_train, y_train, epochs=10, batch_size=32)
```

5. **Evaluation:** After training, evaluate the model's performance on a separate test dataset:

```
test_loss, test_accuracy = model.evaluate(X_test, y_test)
print(f'Test accuracy: {test_accuracy:.4f}')
```

6. **Making Predictions:** You can use the trained model to make predictions on new data:

```
predictions = model.predict(new_data)
```

Customizing the Architecture:

You can customize the architecture by adding more layers, changing activation functions, adjusting the number of neurons, and experimenting with various configurations. The choice of architecture depends on the specific task and dataset you're working with.

Saving and Loading Models:

You can save a trained model to disk and load it later for inference:

```
# Save the model
model.save('my_model.h5')
```

```
# Load the model
loaded_model = keras.models.load_model('my_model.h5')
```

Building neural networks in Python is made straightforward with deep learning libraries like TensorFlow and Keras. You can create complex architectures for various tasks, including image classification, natural language processing, and more. As you become more familiar with neural networks, you can explore advanced concepts like transfer learning, fine-tuning, and building custom layers to address specific challenges in machine learning.

Section 9.3: Convolutional Neural Networks (CNNs)

Convolutional Neural Networks (CNNs) are a class of neural networks designed primarily for processing grid-like data, such as images and video. They are a fundamental component of deep learning in computer vision and have been used in a wide range of applications, including image classification, object detection, image generation, and more.

Key Components of CNNs:

1. Convolutional Layers:

Convolutional layers are the building blocks of CNNs. They apply a set of learnable filters (also known as kernels) to the input data, which allows the network to automatically learn features from the data. Convolutional layers are responsible for capturing spatial hierarchies of features.

2. Pooling Layers:

Pooling layers downsample the output of convolutional layers. Common pooling operations include max-pooling and average-pooling. Pooling helps reduce the spatial dimensions of the data while retaining important features, which leads to better computational efficiency and reduced overfitting.

3. Activation Functions:

Activation functions like ReLU (Rectified Linear Unit) are applied to the output of convolutional and fully connected layers. They introduce non-linearity into the network, enabling it to model complex relationships in the data.

After processing the data through convolutional and pooling layers, CNNs often have one or more fully connected layers (similar to those in feedforward neural networks). These layers are responsible for making predictions based on the features learned by earlier layers.

CNN Architecture:

A typical CNN architecture consists of multiple convolutional layers, followed by pooling layers, and finally fully connected layers. The last layer usually has a softmax activation for classification tasks, while for regression tasks, it may have a linear activation function.

Here's an example of a simple CNN architecture in Keras:

```
model = keras.Sequential([
    keras.layers.Conv2D(32, (3, 3), activation='relu', input_shape=(32, 32, 3
)),  # Convolutional Layer
    keras.layers.MaxPooling2D((2, 2)),  # Max-pooling Layer
    keras.layers.Conv2D(64, (3, 3), activation='relu'),  # Convolutional Laye
r
    keras.layers.MaxPooling2D((2, 2)),  # Max-pooling Layer
    keras.layers.Conv2D(64, (3, 3), activation='relu'),  # Convolutional Laye
r
    keras.layers.Flatten(),  # Flatten the output for fully connected Layers
    keras.layers.Dense(64, activation='relu'),  # Fully connected Layer
    keras.layers.Dense(10, activation='softmax')  # Output Layer with softmax
activation
])
```

Training CNNs:

Training a CNN involves providing labeled training data and using optimization techniques like stochastic gradient descent (SGD) to adjust the network's weights. The choice of loss function depends on the specific task, such as categorical cross-entropy for classification and mean squared error (MSE) for regression.

Transfer Learning:

One of the strengths of CNNs is their ability to perform transfer learning. You can take a pre-trained CNN, remove the final layers, and fine-tune it on a different but related task. This is particularly useful when you have a small dataset but want to leverage the knowledge learned from a large dataset.

Applications of CNNs:

CNNs have revolutionized computer vision and have been applied in various domains:

- **Image Classification:** CNNs excel at categorizing images into predefined classes.
- **Object Detection:** They can identify and locate objects within images.

- **Image Generation:** CNNs are used in generative models like GANs to create realistic images.
- **Face Recognition:** They can recognize and verify faces.
- **Medical Image Analysis:** CNNs help in diagnosing diseases from medical images.
- **Autonomous Vehicles:** They play a crucial role in self-driving cars for object detection and tracking.

In summary, Convolutional Neural Networks have had a profound impact on computer vision tasks and have enabled machines to achieve human-level performance in many visual recognition tasks. Understanding how to design and train CNNs is essential for anyone working on image-related machine learning and deep learning projects.

Section 9.4: Recurrent Neural Networks (RNNs)

Recurrent Neural Networks (RNNs) are a class of neural networks designed to process sequences of data. Unlike feedforward neural networks, RNNs have connections that loop back on themselves, allowing them to maintain a hidden state that captures information about previous time steps. This makes RNNs well-suited for tasks involving sequential data, such as natural language processing (NLP), speech recognition, time series prediction, and more.

Key Components of RNNs:

1. Recurrent Layers:

The core building block of an RNN is the recurrent layer. It allows information to be passed from one step of the sequence to the next by maintaining a hidden state vector. This hidden state captures information about the previous time steps and influences the predictions made at the current time step.

2. Time Steps:

An RNN processes data one time step at a time. Each time step corresponds to one element of the sequence, and the network's hidden state is updated at each time step based on the current input and the previous hidden state.

3. Sequence Length:

The length of the input sequence can vary, making RNNs flexible for handling sequences of different lengths. For example, in NLP, sentences can have varying numbers of words.

4. Recurrent Activation Function:

RNNs use a recurrent activation function, usually a hyperbolic tangent (tanh) or a rectified linear unit (ReLU), to compute the hidden state at each time step. This introduces non-linearity into the network and allows it to capture complex dependencies in the data.

RNN Architectures:

There are different RNN architectures, including:

1. One-to-One (Feedforward) RNN:

This is a traditional feedforward neural network with no recurrence. It processes fixed-size input data and produces fixed-size output.

2. One-to-Many RNN:

In this architecture, the network takes a single input and produces a sequence of outputs. An example is image captioning, where an image is the input, and the network generates a sentence as output.

3. Many-to-One RNN:

This is used for tasks where the network processes a sequence and produces a single output. Sentiment analysis in NLP is an example, where the input is a sequence of words, and the output is a sentiment score.

4. Many-to-Many RNN (Sequence-to-Sequence):

In this architecture, the network takes a sequence as input and produces a sequence as output. Machine translation is a classic example, where a sequence of words in one language is translated into a sequence of words in another language.

Training RNNs:

Training RNNs involves backpropagation through time (BPTT), which is an extension of the standard backpropagation algorithm. BPTT computes gradients with respect to the network's weights by unrolling it through time, effectively treating it as a feedforward neural network with multiple layers corresponding to time steps.

Challenges with RNNs:

RNNs suffer from some limitations, such as the vanishing gradient problem, which makes it difficult for them to capture long-range dependencies in sequences. To address this, variations of RNNs have been developed, including Long Short-Term Memory (LSTM) and Gated Recurrent Unit (GRU), which have been effective at mitigating the vanishing gradient problem.

Applications of RNNs:

RNNs have been applied to a wide range of applications:

- **Natural Language Processing:** They are used for machine translation, text generation, sentiment analysis, and more.
- **Speech Recognition:** RNNs can convert spoken language into text.
- **Time Series Prediction:** RNNs can forecast stock prices, weather, and more.

- **Image Captioning:** They generate textual descriptions for images.
- **Gesture Recognition:** RNNs can recognize hand gestures in video sequences.
- **Autonomous Vehicles:** They help in processing sensor data for self-driving cars.

In summary, Recurrent Neural Networks are a powerful tool for handling sequential data. Understanding their architecture and training techniques is essential for tasks involving sequences, and they have been instrumental in advancing various fields, particularly in natural language processing and time series analysis.

Section 9.5: Deep Learning Applications

Deep learning, a subset of machine learning, has revolutionized many fields and continues to drive advancements in various applications. In this section, we will explore some key deep learning applications and their significance.

1. Computer Vision:

Deep learning has made remarkable strides in computer vision tasks. Convolutional Neural Networks (CNNs) have become the backbone of image classification, object detection, and image segmentation. Applications range from facial recognition and autonomous vehicles to medical image analysis for disease diagnosis.

```python
# Example of using a pre-trained CNN for image classification
import tensorflow as tf
from tensorflow.keras.applications import MobileNetV2
from tensorflow.keras.preprocessing import image
from tensorflow.keras.applications.mobilenet_v2 import preprocess_input, deco
de_predictions

model = MobileNetV2(weights='imagenet')
img_path = 'image.jpg'
img = image.load_img(img_path, target_size=(224, 224))
x = image.img_to_array(img)
x = preprocess_input(x)
x = np.expand_dims(x, axis=0)
predictions = model.predict(x)
decoded_predictions = decode_predictions(predictions, top=3)[0]
print(decoded_predictions)
```

2. Natural Language Processing (NLP):

Deep learning has brought significant advancements to NLP tasks. Transformers, a type of deep learning architecture, have enabled state-of-the-art results in tasks like language translation, sentiment analysis, chatbots, and text summarization.

```python
# Example of using a pre-trained Transformer model for text classification
from transformers import pipeline
```

```
classifier = pipeline('sentiment-analysis')
text = "I enjoyed the movie; it was fantastic!"
result = classifier(text)
print(result)
```

3. Reinforcement Learning:

Deep reinforcement learning has made breakthroughs in training agents to make decisions and take actions in environments. This has practical applications in robotics, game playing, and autonomous systems.

```
# Example of training a Deep Q-Network (DQN) agent using TensorFlow
import tensorflow as tf
import gym
from stable_baselines3 import DQN

env = gym.make("CartPole-v1")
model = DQN("MlpPolicy", env, verbose=1)
model.learn(total_timesteps=10000)
model.save("dqn_cartpole")
```

4. Healthcare:

Deep learning is transforming healthcare with applications in medical image analysis, disease diagnosis, drug discovery, and predicting patient outcomes. Convolutional neural networks can identify abnormalities in medical images, while recurrent neural networks can analyze patient data over time.

```
# Example of using deep learning for medical image analysis
import tensorflow as tf
from tensorflow.keras.applications import ResNet50
from tensorflow.keras.preprocessing import image
from tensorflow.keras.applications.resnet50 import preprocess_input, decode_p
redictions

model = ResNet50(weights='imagenet')
img_path = 'medical_image.jpg'
img = image.load_img(img_path, target_size=(224, 224))
x = image.img_to_array(img)
x = preprocess_input(x)
x = np.expand_dims(x, axis=0)
predictions = model.predict(x)
decoded_predictions = decode_predictions(predictions, top=3)[0]
print(decoded_predictions)
```

5. Autonomous Vehicles:

Deep learning plays a crucial role in autonomous vehicles, enabling perception, decision-making, and control. Neural networks process sensor data, identify objects and obstacles, and make real-time driving decisions.

```python
# Example of using deep learning for object detection in autonomous vehicles
import tensorflow as tf
from object_detection.utils import visualization_utils as viz_utils

# Load a pre-trained object detection model
model = tf.saved_model.load('object_detection_model')
# Process camera feed and detect objects
input_image = capture_camera_feed()
detections = model(input_image)
# Visualize the detections
viz_utils.visualize_boxes_and_labels_on_image_array(
    input_image[0], detections['detection_boxes'][0].numpy(),
    detections['detection_classes'][0].numpy().astype(int),
    detections['detection_scores'][0].numpy(),
    category_index, use_normalized_coordinates=True,
    max_boxes_to_draw=200, min_score_thresh=0.30)
```

These examples showcase the broad impact of deep learning across various domains. As deep learning models continue to advance, we can expect even more breakthroughs in these and other fields, paving the way for exciting new applications and discoveries.

Chapter 10: Natural Language Processing with Python

Section 10.1: Text Preprocessing and Tokenization

Text preprocessing is a critical step in natural language processing (NLP) tasks. It involves cleaning and transforming raw text data into a format that can be easily understood and analyzed by machine learning models. One of the primary tasks in text preprocessing is tokenization, which is the process of splitting text into smaller units called tokens. This section explores the importance of text preprocessing and provides an overview of tokenization techniques.

Why Text Preprocessing?

Text data, especially when obtained from various sources, can be noisy and unstructured. Text preprocessing helps in:

1. **Noise Reduction**: Removing irrelevant characters, symbols, and special characters that don't contribute to the analysis.

2. **Normalization**: Converting text to lowercase to ensure uniformity and consistency in the data.

3. **Stopword Removal**: Eliminating common words (e.g., "the," "and," "in") that carry little semantic meaning.

4. **Tokenization**: Breaking text into individual words or subword units for analysis.

Tokenization Techniques

Tokenization is a fundamental step in NLP. Different techniques can be used, depending on the specific requirements of the task. Here are some common tokenization methods:

1. Word Tokenization:

Word tokenization breaks text into words based on spaces or punctuation. It's suitable for many NLP tasks, including text classification and sentiment analysis.

```
import nltk
from nltk.tokenize import word_tokenize

text = "Natural language processing is a subfield of artificial intelligence.
"
tokens = word_tokenize(text)
print(tokens)
```

2. Sentence Tokenization:

Sentence tokenization divides text into sentences. This is useful when you want to analyze text at the sentence level.

```
from nltk.tokenize import sent_tokenize

text = "NLP has applications in machine translation, text summarization, and
more. It's a fascinating field."
sentences = sent_tokenize(text)
print(sentences)
```

3. Subword Tokenization:

Subword tokenization, often used for languages with complex morphology, splits text into smaller units like subword pieces. This is beneficial for machine translation and speech recognition.

```
from tokenizers import Tokenizer, models, trainers, pre_tokenizers, decoders

tokenizer = Tokenizer(models.BPE())
trainer = trainers.BpeTrainer(special_tokens=["[PAD]", "[CLS]", "[SEP]", "[MA
SK]", "[UNK]"])
tokenizer.pre_tokenizer = pre_tokenizers.ByteLevel()
tokenizer.decoder = decoders.ByteLevel()
files = ["text_file1.txt", "text_file2.txt"]
tokenizer.train(files, trainer)
encoded = tokenizer.encode("Machine learning is fascinating.")
print(encoded.tokens)
```

Conclusion

Text preprocessing, including tokenization, is a critical step in preparing text data for NLP tasks. The choice of tokenization method depends on the specific requirements of the task and the characteristics of the text data. Clean and well-tokenized text data lays the foundation for building effective NLP models and extracting valuable insights from text.

Section 10.2: Building Text Classification Models

In the field of Natural Language Processing (NLP), text classification is one of the most common and valuable tasks. It involves assigning predefined categories or labels to text documents. Text classification finds applications in spam detection, sentiment analysis, topic categorization, and more. In this section, we will explore the process of building text classification models using Python and popular libraries like scikit-learn.

Data Preparation

Before diving into building text classification models, you need to prepare your data. Typically, your dataset should consist of labeled text documents. Each document should be associated with a category or label. You'll want to split your data into training and testing sets to evaluate the model's performance.

```
from sklearn.model_selection import train_test_split

# Assuming you have a dataset with 'text' and 'label' columns
X_train, X_test, y_train, y_test = train_test_split(data['text'], data['label'], test_size=0.2, random_state=42)
```

Text Vectorization

Machine learning models work with numerical data, so you need to convert your text data into numerical form. This process is called text vectorization. Two common techniques are:

1. **Bag of Words (BoW)**: In BoW, each document is represented as a vector where each dimension corresponds to a unique word in the entire corpus. The value in each dimension represents the word's frequency or presence in the document.

```
from sklearn.feature_extraction.text import CountVectorizer

vectorizer = CountVectorizer()
X_train_bow = vectorizer.fit_transform(X_train)
X_test_bow = vectorizer.transform(X_test)
```

2. **TF-IDF (Term Frequency-Inverse Document Frequency)**: TF-IDF considers not only the term frequency but also the importance of the term in the entire corpus. It helps in identifying words that are discriminative for classification.

```
from sklearn.feature_extraction.text import TfidfVectorizer

tfidf_vectorizer = TfidfVectorizer()
X_train_tfidf = tfidf_vectorizer.fit_transform(X_train)
X_test_tfidf = tfidf_vectorizer.transform(X_test)
```

Model Selection

You can use various machine learning algorithms for text classification. Common choices include:

- **Naive Bayes**: A simple and effective algorithm for text classification.

```
from sklearn.naive_bayes import MultinomialNB

nb_classifier = MultinomialNB()
nb_classifier.fit(X_train_bow, y_train)
```

- **Support Vector Machine (SVM)**: SVMs are known for their robust performance in text classification.

```
from sklearn.svm import SVC

svm_classifier = SVC()
svm_classifier.fit(X_train_tfidf, y_train)
```

- **Deep Learning**: Deep learning models like Convolutional Neural Networks (CNNs) and Recurrent Neural Networks (RNNs) can also be used for text classification, especially for complex tasks.

```
# Example of using a simple CNN for text classification with TensorFlow/Keras
from tensorflow.keras.models import Sequential
from tensorflow.keras.layers import Embedding, Conv1D, GlobalMaxPooling1D, Dense

model = Sequential()
model.add(Embedding(input_dim=vocab_size, output_dim=embedding_dim, input_length=max_length))
model.add(Conv1D(128, 5, activation='relu'))
model.add(GlobalMaxPooling1D())
model.add(Dense(1, activation='sigmoid'))
model.compile(optimizer='adam', loss='binary_crossentropy', metrics=['accuracy'])
model.fit(X_train, y_train, epochs=5, batch_size=64, validation_data=(X_test, y_test))
```

Model Evaluation

Once you have trained your text classification model, you should evaluate its performance using metrics like accuracy, precision, recall, and F1-score.

```
from sklearn.metrics import accuracy_score, classification_report

y_pred = nb_classifier.predict(X_test_bow)
accuracy = accuracy_score(y_test, y_pred)
classification_rep = classification_report(y_test, y_pred)
print(f"Accuracy: {accuracy:.2f}")
print(classification_rep)
```

Conclusion

Text classification is a valuable NLP task with numerous real-world applications. By following the steps outlined in this section, you can build text classification models that effectively categorize text documents based on predefined labels. Keep in mind that the choice of data preprocessing techniques, text vectorization methods, and machine learning algorithms should align with the specific characteristics and requirements of your text classification problem.

Section 10.3: Word Embeddings (Word2Vec, GloVe)

Word embeddings are a crucial component of modern Natural Language Processing (NLP) models. They represent words as dense vectors in a continuous vector space, capturing semantic relationships between words. Word embeddings have revolutionized the way we handle textual data and are widely used in various NLP tasks like text classification, sentiment analysis, and machine translation. In this section, we'll explore two popular word embedding techniques: Word2Vec and GloVe.

Word2Vec

Word2Vec is a word embedding model developed by Google. It learns to represent words as vectors in such a way that words with similar meanings are closer in the vector space. The Word2Vec model comes in two flavors: Continuous Bag of Words (CBOW) and Skip-gram.

Training Word2Vec Models

To train a Word2Vec model, you can use libraries like Gensim in Python. Here's an example of training a Word2Vec model on a corpus of text:

```python
from gensim.models import Word2Vec

# Example corpus (a list of sentences)
corpus = [["I", "love", "machine", "learning"], ["Word", "embeddings", "are",
"useful"]]

# Train Word2Vec model
model = Word2Vec(sentences=corpus, vector_size=100, window=5, sg=0)  # sg=0 f
or CBOW, sg=1 for Skip-gram
```

Once the model is trained, you can obtain word vectors:

```python
vector = model.wv['machine']
```

GloVe (Global Vectors for Word Representation)

GloVe is another popular word embedding technique that is based on a global matrix factorization approach. It leverages global word co-occurrence statistics to generate word vectors. Pre-trained GloVe word vectors are available for download, making it easy to use in various NLP tasks.

Using Pre-trained GloVe Vectors

You can use pre-trained GloVe word vectors in your NLP models. Here's how to load pre-trained GloVe vectors using Python:

```
from gensim.scripts.glove2word2vec import glove2word2vec
from gensim.models import KeyedVectors

# Convert GloVe format to Word2Vec format
glove_input_file = 'glove.6B.100d.txt'
word2vec_output_file = 'glove.6B.100d.word2vec'
glove2word2vec(glove_input_file, word2vec_output_file)

# Load pre-trained GloVe word vectors
glove_model = KeyedVectors.load_word2vec_format(word2vec_output_file, binary=
False)
```

Now you can access word vectors in the GloVe model:

```
vector = glove_model['machine']
```

Application of Word Embeddings

Word embeddings are widely used in NLP tasks. For example, in text classification, you can use pre-trained word embeddings as input features for a neural network:

```
from tensorflow.keras.models import Sequential
from tensorflow.keras.layers import Embedding, Flatten, Dense

# Example model using pre-trained GloVe embeddings
model = Sequential()
model.add(Embedding(input_dim=vocab_size, output_dim=embedding_dim, input_len
gth=max_length, weights=[embedding_matrix], trainable=False))
model.add(Flatten())
model.add(Dense(1, activation='sigmoid'))
model.compile(optimizer='adam', loss='binary_crossentropy', metrics=['accurac
y'])
```

In this example, `embedding_matrix` contains the pre-trained GloVe word vectors for your vocabulary.

Word embeddings have significantly improved the performance of NLP models by capturing semantic relationships between words, making them an essential tool for anyone working with textual data in machine learning and natural language processing.

Conclusion

Word embeddings like Word2Vec and GloVe have revolutionized the field of Natural Language Processing by providing a way to represent words as dense vectors in a continuous vector space. These embeddings capture semantic relationships between words and are crucial for various NLP tasks. Whether you train your own Word2Vec model or use pre-trained GloVe vectors, word embeddings play a vital role in enhancing the performance of NLP models.

Section 10.4: Sequence-to-Sequence Models

Sequence-to-sequence (Seq2Seq) models are a class of neural networks used for various natural language processing tasks that involve input and output sequences of different lengths. These models are particularly useful for tasks like machine translation, text summarization, and chatbot development. In this section, we'll explore the architecture and application of sequence-to-sequence models.

Architecture of Seq2Seq Models

Seq2Seq models consist of two main components: an encoder and a decoder. The encoder processes the input sequence and encodes it into a fixed-size context vector, which captures the input's information. The decoder takes this context vector and generates the output sequence.

Encoder

The encoder is typically a recurrent neural network (RNN), a long short-term memory (LSTM), or a gated recurrent unit (GRU). It processes the input sequence one step at a time and maintains a hidden state that summarizes the information seen so far. At the end of the input sequence, the hidden state serves as the context vector.

Decoder

The decoder is another RNN or LSTM that takes the context vector from the encoder as its initial state. It generates the output sequence one step at a time, often using a softmax activation function to produce a probability distribution over possible output tokens at each step. The decoder can also incorporate attention mechanisms to focus on different parts of the input sequence while generating the output.

Applications of Seq2Seq Models

1. **Machine Translation**: Seq2Seq models have been highly successful in machine translation tasks, such as translating English sentences to French or vice versa. The encoder processes the source language, and the decoder generates the target language.

2. **Text Summarization**: These models are used to summarize long articles or documents into shorter, coherent summaries. The input is the full text, and the output is a concise summary.

3. **Chatbots**: Seq2Seq models are employed in building chatbots that can generate human-like responses to user inputs. The encoder processes the user's message, and the decoder generates the chatbot's response.

4. **Speech Recognition**: In automatic speech recognition, Seq2Seq models can convert spoken language into written text. The input is the audio signal, and the output is the transcribed text.

Example Code

Here's a simplified example of training a Seq2Seq model for machine translation using the Keras library in Python:

```python
from tensorflow.keras.models import Sequential
from tensorflow.keras.layers import Embedding, LSTM, Dense

# Define the encoder
encoder = Sequential()
encoder.add(Embedding(input_dim=source_vocab_size, output_dim=embedding_dim,
input_length=max_source_length))
encoder.add(LSTM(units=hidden_units, return_state=True))

# Define the decoder
decoder = Sequential()
decoder.add(Embedding(input_dim=target_vocab_size, output_dim=embedding_dim,
input_length=max_target_length))
decoder.add(LSTM(units=hidden_units, return_sequences=True, return_state=True
))
decoder.add(Dense(target_vocab_size, activation='softmax'))

# Connect the encoder and decoder
encoder_inputs = Input(shape=(max_source_length,))
encoder_outputs, state_h, state_c = encoder(encoder_inputs)
encoder_states = [state_h, state_c]

decoder_inputs = Input(shape=(max_target_length,))
decoder_outputs, _, _ = decoder(decoder_inputs, initial_state=encoder_states)

# Compile and train the model
model = Model([encoder_inputs, decoder_inputs], decoder_outputs)
model.compile(optimizer='adam', loss='categorical_crossentropy', metrics=['ac
curacy'])
model.fit([encoder_input_data, decoder_input_data], decoder_target_data, batc
h_size=batch_size, epochs=epochs, validation_split=0.2)
```

In this example, encoder_input_data, decoder_input_data, and decoder_target_data would be your training data for machine translation.

Seq2Seq models have shown remarkable performance in various sequence-to-sequence tasks and continue to be an active area of research in natural language processing. They enable machines to understand and generate human-like text, making them a crucial tool in modern NLP applications.

Section 10.5: Sentiment Analysis and Text Generation

Sentiment analysis, also known as opinion mining, is a natural language processing (NLP) technique that involves determining the sentiment or emotional tone expressed in a piece of text. On the other hand, text generation focuses on the automatic creation of coherent and contextually relevant text based on a given input or prompt. In this section, we'll explore both sentiment analysis and text generation techniques and their applications.

Sentiment Analysis

Overview

Sentiment analysis aims to classify text as positive, negative, or neutral based on the emotional content of the text. It has a wide range of applications, including:

- **Social Media Monitoring**: Analyzing user-generated content on platforms like Twitter and Facebook to understand public sentiment toward products, brands, or events.
- **Customer Feedback Analysis**: Automatically categorizing customer reviews as positive, negative, or neutral to assess product or service quality.
- **Market Research**: Analyzing textual data from surveys, focus groups, and online forums to gain insights into consumer opinions and preferences.

Techniques

Sentiment analysis can be performed using various techniques, including:

- **Lexicon-Based Approaches**: These methods rely on sentiment lexicons or dictionaries containing words with pre-assigned sentiment scores. Text is scored based on the sentiment of the words it contains.
- **Machine Learning Models**: Supervised machine learning models, such as support vector machines (SVM), recurrent neural networks (RNNs), or transformers, can be trained on labeled sentiment datasets to predict sentiment.
- **Deep Learning Models**: Models like convolutional neural networks (CNNs) and transformers have achieved state-of-the-art performance in sentiment analysis tasks by capturing complex patterns in text data.

Text Generation

Overview

Text generation involves generating coherent and contextually relevant text based on a given input or prompt. It can be used for various applications, including:

- **Chatbots**: Generating human-like responses in chatbot interactions with users.
- **Content Creation**: Automatically generating articles, stories, or creative content.

- **Language Translation**: Generating translations of text from one language to another.
- **Code Generation**: Automatically generating code based on high-level descriptions.

Techniques

Text generation can be achieved through different techniques, including:

- **Recurrent Neural Networks (RNNs)**: RNNs, particularly LSTM and GRU variants, can be used for sequential data generation tasks, including text generation.
- **Markov Models**: Markov models, such as n-grams or Hidden Markov Models (HMMs), are probabilistic models used for generating text by predicting the next word based on the previous words.
- **Transformer-Based Models**: Large-scale transformer models, like GPT (Generative Pre-trained Transformer), have achieved remarkable results in text generation tasks. These models can generate coherent and contextually relevant text across various domains.

Example Code

Here's a simplified example of sentiment analysis using Python's Natural Language Toolkit (NLTK):

```python
import nltk
from nltk.sentiment.vader import SentimentIntensityAnalyzer

# Initialize the sentiment analyzer
nltk.download('vader_lexicon')
analyzer = SentimentIntensityAnalyzer()

# Analyze sentiment
text = "I love this product! It's amazing."
sentiment_scores = analyzer.polarity_scores(text)

# Interpret sentiment scores
if sentiment_scores['compound'] >= 0.05:
    sentiment = 'positive'
elif sentiment_scores['compound'] <= -0.05:
    sentiment = 'negative'
else:
    sentiment = 'neutral'

print(f'Sentiment: {sentiment}')
```

And here's an example of text generation using the GPT-3 model via the OpenAI API:

```python
import openai

# Set up your API key and endpoint
```

```python
api_key = 'YOUR_API_KEY'
openai.api_key = api_key

# Prompt for text generation
prompt = "Once upon a time in a"
response = openai.Completion.create(
    engine="text-davinci-002",
    prompt=prompt,
    max_tokens=50
)

generated_text = response.choices[0].text
print(generated_text)
```

These examples demonstrate the basic implementation of sentiment analysis and text generation using popular NLP libraries and models. Sentiment analysis and text generation are essential techniques for understanding and generating textual content, and they find applications in various domains, including customer service, content generation, and creative writing.

Chapter 11: Computer Vision with Python

Section 11.1: Image Data Handling in Python

In this section, we will explore the fundamentals of handling image data in Python, which is an essential skill for computer vision tasks. Computer vision involves the processing and analysis of visual information from the world, typically in the form of images or videos. Whether you're building an image classification model, object detection system, or any other computer vision application, you need to understand how to work with image data effectively.

Importing Required Libraries

To get started, let's import some common libraries for working with image data in Python. The two primary libraries for image handling are OpenCV (Open Source Computer Vision Library) and Pillow (Python Imaging Library, known as PIL). You can install these libraries using pip if you haven't already:

```
!pip install opencv-python-headless pillow
```

Now, let's import these libraries:

```python
import cv2
from PIL import Image
import numpy as np
```

Loading and Displaying Images

The first step in any computer vision task is to load and display images. You can load images using OpenCV's imread function or Pillow's Image.open function. Let's see examples of both:

```
# Using OpenCV to load an image
image_cv2 = cv2.imread('image.jpg')

# Using Pillow to load an image
image_pillow = Image.open('image.jpg')
```

You can display the loaded images using OpenCV's imshow function or Pillow's show method:

```
# Displaying an image using OpenCV
cv2.imshow('OpenCV Image', image_cv2)
cv2.waitKey(0)
cv2.destroyAllWindows()

# Displaying an image using Pillow
image_pillow.show()
```

Converting Between OpenCV and Pillow

Sometimes, you may need to convert images between OpenCV and Pillow formats. Here's how you can do it:

```
# Convert from OpenCV to Pillow
image_cv2 = cv2.cvtColor(image_cv2, cv2.COLOR_BGR2RGB)
image_pillow = Image.fromarray(image_cv2)

# Convert from Pillow to OpenCV
image_cv2 = np.array(image_pillow)
```

Basic Image Operations

Once you have loaded an image, you can perform various operations on it, such as resizing, cropping, and rotating. Here are some common operations:

```
# Resize an image using Pillow
resized_image = image_pillow.resize((width, height))

# Crop a region of interest (ROI) from an image using Pillow
roi = image_pillow.crop((left, upper, right, lower))

# Rotate an image using Pillow
rotated_image = image_pillow.rotate(angle)
```

These are the basic image handling operations you need to be familiar with when working with computer vision tasks. In the upcoming sections, we will delve deeper into specific computer vision topics, including image classification, object detection, and more.

Section 11.2: Image Classification

Image classification is one of the fundamental tasks in computer vision, where the goal is to assign a label or category to an input image. In this section, we will explore the concept of image classification, the techniques involved, and how to implement it using Python and popular deep learning frameworks like TensorFlow and PyTorch.

Understanding Image Classification

Image classification involves training a model to recognize and categorize objects or patterns within images. It's a supervised learning task where the model is trained on a dataset of labeled images, where each image is associated with a specific class or category.

The process typically involves the following steps:

1. **Data Collection**: Gather a dataset of images, where each image is labeled with its corresponding class or category. For example, if you're building a model to classify animals, you might have images of cats, dogs, birds, etc.

2. **Data Preprocessing**: Prepare the data by resizing images to a uniform size, normalizing pixel values, and splitting the dataset into training and testing sets.

3. **Model Selection**: Choose an appropriate neural network architecture for image classification. Convolutional Neural Networks (CNNs) are commonly used for this task due to their ability to capture spatial hierarchies in images.

4. **Model Training**: Train the selected model on the training data, adjusting the model's weights and biases to minimize the classification error.

5. **Model Evaluation**: Evaluate the trained model's performance on a separate testing dataset to assess its accuracy and other metrics.

6. **Inference**: Use the trained model to make predictions on new, unlabeled images.

Implementing Image Classification

Here's a high-level overview of implementing image classification using Python and deep learning frameworks:

1. Data Preparation

The first step is to prepare your dataset. You can use libraries like TensorFlow Datasets, PyTorch's torchvision, or manually collect and label your data. Ensure that you have a training set and a separate validation/testing set.

2. Data Augmentation (Optional)

Data augmentation techniques like random rotations, flips, and translations can be applied to increase the diversity of your training data and improve model generalization.

3. Model Building

Choose a pre-trained CNN architecture (e.g., VGG, ResNet, Inception) or design your own. In many cases, transfer learning can be used, where you fine-tune a pre-trained model on your specific dataset.

4. Model Training

Train your model using the training dataset. During training, the model's weights are adjusted using optimization techniques like gradient descent. Monitor training progress and validation performance to prevent overfitting.

```
# Example code for training a model using TensorFlow and Keras
model.compile(optimizer='adam', loss='categorical_crossentropy', metrics=['accuracy'])
model.fit(train_dataset, epochs=epochs, validation_data=validation_dataset)
```

5. Model Evaluation

Evaluate the trained model on the validation/testing dataset to measure its performance. Common evaluation metrics include accuracy, precision, recall, and F1-score.

```
# Example code for evaluating a model
loss, accuracy = model.evaluate(test_dataset)
```

6. Inference

Once your model is trained and evaluated, you can use it to make predictions on new, unlabeled images.

```
# Example code for making predictions
predictions = model.predict(new_images)
```

Conclusion

Image classification is a critical task in computer vision, with applications ranging from object recognition to medical diagnosis. It involves data collection, preprocessing, model building, training, evaluation, and inference. Deep learning frameworks like TensorFlow and PyTorch have made it more accessible to implement image classification models effectively. In the next section, we will delve into the world of word embeddings and natural language processing.

Section 11.3: Object Detection and Localization

Object detection and localization are fundamental tasks in computer vision that involve identifying and locating objects within images or videos. Unlike image classification, which assigns a single label to an entire image, object detection identifies and precisely localizes multiple objects within an image, often by drawing bounding boxes around them. This section explores the concepts, techniques, and tools used in object detection and localization.

Understanding Object Detection

Object detection tasks involve two primary objectives:

1. **Object Classification**: Identifying the class or category of each object present in an image. This is similar to image classification but is performed separately for each object.

2. **Object Localization**: Determining the location of each object in the image by drawing bounding boxes around them. These bounding boxes provide information about the object's position and size.

Object detection has numerous real-world applications, such as:

- Autonomous vehicles detecting pedestrians and other vehicles on the road.
- Surveillance systems identifying intruders or suspicious activities.
- Healthcare systems locating and analyzing tumors in medical images.
- Retail systems tracking products and monitoring inventory.

Techniques for Object Detection

Several techniques have been developed for object detection, each with its strengths and weaknesses. Some common approaches include:

1. **Traditional Computer Vision Methods**: These methods rely on handcrafted features and algorithms to detect objects. Examples include Haar cascades and Histogram of Oriented Gradients (HOG) combined with support vector machines (SVM).

2. **Deep Learning-Based Methods**: Deep learning has revolutionized object detection. Convolutional Neural Networks (CNNs) play a crucial role in modern object detection techniques. Some popular architectures for object detection include:

   - **Faster R-CNN**: Combines region proposal networks (RPNs) with CNNs for improved accuracy and speed.
   - **YOLO (You Only Look Once)**: Divides the image into a grid and predicts bounding boxes and class probabilities for each grid cell simultaneously.

- **SSD (Single Shot MultiBox Detector)**: Similar to YOLO but uses a series of convolutional layers to predict bounding boxes at multiple scales.

Implementing Object Detection

Implementing object detection typically involves the following steps:

1. **Data Collection**: Gather a labeled dataset containing images with object annotations (bounding boxes and corresponding class labels).

2. **Data Preprocessing**: Prepare the data by resizing images, normalizing pixel values, and augmenting the dataset with techniques like data augmentation.

3. **Model Selection**: Choose a pre-trained object detection model or create a custom one using deep learning frameworks like TensorFlow, PyTorch, or OpenCV.

4. **Model Training**: Fine-tune the selected model on your dataset, adjusting its weights to improve object detection accuracy.

5. **Inference**: Use the trained model to detect and localize objects in new images or videos.

6. **Post-processing**: Apply non-maximum suppression to remove redundant bounding boxes and refine the final object detections.

Object Detection Tools

Several libraries and frameworks simplify object detection implementation. Some popular ones include:

- **TensorFlow Object Detection API**: A collection of pre-trained models and tools for object detection tasks.
- **PyTorch TorchVision**: Part of the PyTorch library, TorchVision provides pre-trained object detection models and utilities.
- **OpenCV**: A versatile computer vision library that offers object detection capabilities.
- **YOLOv5**: A popular YOLO-based model for object detection with a focus on simplicity and performance.

Object detection and localization continue to advance, with new models and techniques regularly emerging. These advancements enable a wide range of applications across various industries, making object detection an essential computer vision task. In the next section, we will explore transfer learning, a technique that leverages pre-trained models to solve complex tasks more efficiently.

Section 11.4: Transfer Learning with Pretrained Models

Transfer learning is a powerful technique in deep learning and computer vision that allows us to leverage the knowledge learned from one task to improve performance on another related task. In the context of object detection and computer vision, transfer learning involves using pretrained models, typically trained on large datasets for tasks like image classification, as a starting point for object detection tasks. This section explores the concept of transfer learning in object detection and how pretrained models can be utilized effectively.

The Motivation for Transfer Learning

Transfer learning is motivated by the idea that models trained on large and diverse datasets have learned valuable features and representations that are useful for a wide range of computer vision tasks. Instead of training an object detection model from scratch, which can be data and resource-intensive, we can start with a pretrained model and fine-tune it for our specific task. This approach offers several advantages:

1. **Reduced Training Time**: Pretrained models have already learned generic features, so fine-tuning requires less time and data compared to training from scratch.

2. **Improved Performance**: Transfer learning often leads to better object detection performance, especially when you have limited labeled data for your specific task.

3. **Generalization**: Pretrained models capture general features like edges, textures, and object parts, which can be valuable for various object detection tasks.

Fine-Tuning Pretrained Models

Fine-tuning a pretrained model for object detection typically involves the following steps:

1. **Choose a Pretrained Model**: Select a pretrained model that is suitable for your task. Common choices include models like VGG16, ResNet, Inception, or MobileNet, which have been pretrained on large-scale image classification datasets.

2. **Modify the Model**: Remove the original classification head (the final fully connected layers) and replace it with new layers that match the number of classes and object detection requirements for your task.

3. **Freeze Pretrained Layers**: Optionally, you can choose to freeze some of the pretrained layers. This means that these layers will not be updated during training, which can be beneficial when you have a limited amount of labeled data.

4. **Dataset Preparation**: Organize your object detection dataset, including annotations with bounding boxes and class labels.

5. **Data Augmentation**: Apply data augmentation techniques to increase the diversity of your training data and improve model robustness.

6. **Training**: Train the modified model on your object detection dataset. During training, the model learns to detect and localize objects within images.

7. **Fine-Tuning Parameters**: Adjust hyperparameters like learning rate, batch size, and the number of training epochs based on your specific task and dataset.

8. **Evaluation**: After training, evaluate the model's performance on a validation or test set to assess its object detection capabilities.

Popular Object Detection Frameworks

Several popular object detection frameworks and libraries support transfer learning with pretrained models, making it accessible to a wide range of developers and researchers. Some of these include:

-   **TensorFlow Object Detection API**: Provides a collection of pretrained models and tools for object detection tasks within TensorFlow.
-   **PyTorch TorchVision**: Part of the PyTorch library, TorchVision offers pretrained models and utilities for object detection.
-   **Detectron2**: Developed by Facebook AI Research (FAIR), Detectron2 is a powerful object detection library built on PyTorch that supports transfer learning and custom model development.

Transfer learning with pretrained models has democratized object detection and made it more accessible for various applications, from self-driving cars to medical image analysis. It allows practitioners to build accurate object detection systems even with limited labeled data and resources. In the next section, we will explore advanced computer vision applications, showcasing the practical impact of these technologies in real-world scenarios.

Section 11.5: Advanced Computer Vision Applications

Computer vision has evolved rapidly over the years, enabling a wide range of advanced applications across various industries. In this section, we'll explore some of the cutting-edge computer vision applications that are transforming fields such as healthcare, autonomous vehicles, agriculture, and more. These applications leverage deep learning, object detection, image segmentation, and other computer vision techniques to solve complex real-world problems.

1. Medical Image Analysis

In healthcare, computer vision is being used for medical image analysis. This includes the detection and diagnosis of diseases from medical images such as X-rays, CT scans, and MRIs. Convolutional neural networks (CNNs) are used to identify anomalies and assist healthcare professionals in making more accurate diagnoses. For example, AI models can detect tumors, fractures, and other abnormalities in medical images.

2. Autonomous Vehicles

Self-driving cars rely heavily on computer vision systems to navigate and make decisions in real-time. Cameras, LiDAR, and other sensors capture data from the vehicle's surroundings, and deep learning models process this data to detect objects, pedestrians, road signs, and lane markings. These systems enable autonomous vehicles to perceive their environment and safely navigate through traffic.

3. Agriculture and Precision Farming

Computer vision is used in agriculture to enhance crop management and yield prediction. Drones equipped with cameras and AI algorithms can monitor crop health, detect diseases, and optimize irrigation. This technology helps farmers make data-driven decisions to increase productivity while conserving resources.

4. Retail and E-commerce

In the retail industry, computer vision powers applications like cashierless stores, where customers can pick up items and walk out without going through a traditional checkout process. Visual search allows users to search for products using images, making online shopping more convenient. Computer vision can also be used to monitor store shelves for inventory management.

5. Security and Surveillance

Surveillance systems use computer vision to detect suspicious activities, identify intruders, and track objects in real-time. Facial recognition technology is used for access control and security authentication. These systems enhance security in public places, airports, and sensitive facilities.

6. Augmented Reality (AR) and Virtual Reality (VR)

AR and VR applications rely on computer vision to track the user's environment and integrate virtual objects seamlessly into the real world. This technology is used in gaming, training simulations, architectural visualization, and more.

7. Environmental Monitoring

Environmental scientists use computer vision to monitor and analyze changes in natural landscapes. This includes tracking deforestation, glacier movement, wildlife populations, and climate patterns. These insights help in environmental conservation efforts.

8. Quality Control and Manufacturing

Computer vision systems are integrated into manufacturing processes to inspect products for defects, ensuring high-quality production. Robots equipped with vision systems can perform tasks like picking and placing objects on assembly lines.

These advanced computer vision applications demonstrate the wide-reaching impact of this technology on diverse industries. As computer vision continues to advance, it holds the potential to revolutionize many aspects of our lives, from healthcare and transportation to entertainment and agriculture. Innovations in algorithms, hardware, and data collection are driving the rapid development of computer vision solutions, making them increasingly accessible and effective.

Chapter 12: Time Series Analysis and Forecasting

Time series data is a type of data where observations are collected or recorded at regular time intervals. This data format is prevalent in various domains, including finance, economics, climate science, and more. Time series analysis and forecasting are essential tools for extracting insights, making predictions, and understanding temporal patterns in data.

Section 12.1: Time Series Data Handling

Before diving into time series analysis and forecasting techniques, it's crucial to understand how to handle time series data effectively. This section will cover the basics of time series data, including data visualization, indexing, and manipulation.

What is Time Series Data?

Time series data consists of observations or measurements recorded at distinct time points or intervals. These data points are typically collected in chronological order, making time a critical component of the dataset. Time series data can be univariate (one variable measured over time) or multivariate (multiple variables measured over time).

Time Series Data Components

Time series data often exhibits specific components that contribute to its overall behavior:

1. **Trend**: The long-term movement or pattern in the data. Trends can be increasing (upward), decreasing (downward), or stable.

2. **Seasonality**: Regular, repeating patterns or cycles in the data. Seasonal patterns often occur at fixed intervals, such as daily, monthly, or yearly.

3. **Noise**: Random fluctuations or irregularities in the data that cannot be attributed to the trend or seasonality. Noise represents the unpredictable aspects of the time series.

Data Visualization

Visualizing time series data is essential for gaining insights and identifying patterns. Common plots for visualizing time series data include line plots, scatter plots, and histograms. Time series decomposition, which separates data into its trend, seasonal, and residual components, is also a valuable visualization technique.

Time Indexing

To perform meaningful analysis on time series data, it's essential to set the time variable as the index of the dataset. This allows for easy time-based slicing and referencing of data points.

Data preprocessing in time series analysis involves tasks such as handling missing values, smoothing noisy data, and transforming data to stabilize variance or make it more stationary. Stationarity is a crucial concept in time series analysis, as many models assume that data is stationary, meaning statistical properties do not change over time.

Python offers several libraries for working with time series data, including:

- **pandas**: For data manipulation and time series indexing.
- **NumPy**: For numerical operations and calculations.
- **Matplotlib** and **Seaborn**: For data visualization.
- **Statsmodels**: For statistical analysis and modeling.
- **Prophet**: An open-source forecasting tool by Facebook for time series forecasting.

In the subsequent sections of this chapter, we will delve deeper into various time series analysis techniques, forecasting methods, and models to extract valuable insights from time series data and make future predictions. Time series analysis is a valuable skill in data science and has numerous practical applications, making it an important topic to explore.

Section 12.2: Time Series Decomposition

Time series decomposition is a fundamental technique used to break down a time series dataset into its individual components: trend, seasonality, and noise. This decomposition process is essential for understanding the underlying patterns and characteristics within time series data. In this section, we will explore the concept of time series decomposition and how to apply it using Python.

Time series decomposition aims to separate a time series into three main components:

1. **Trend**: The long-term movement or pattern in the data. Trends can be upward (indicating growth), downward (indicating a decline), or stable.

2. **Seasonality**: Regular, repeating patterns or cycles in the data. Seasonal patterns often occur at fixed intervals, such as daily, monthly, or yearly. Identifying seasonality is crucial for understanding when certain events or behaviors tend to repeat.

3. **Residuals (Noise)**: The remaining, unexplained part of the data after removing the trend and seasonality components. Residuals represent random fluctuations or irregularities in the data that cannot be attributed to the trend or seasonality. Analyzing residuals can help identify unusual events or anomalies.

Time series decomposition can be performed using two primary methods: additive and multiplicative decomposition.

- **Additive Decomposition**: In additive decomposition, the components (trend, seasonality, and residuals) are combined by adding them together. This method is suitable when the magnitude of seasonality does not depend on the level of the time series.

- **Multiplicative Decomposition**: In multiplicative decomposition, the components are combined by multiplying them. This method is appropriate when the magnitude of seasonality varies with the level of the time series. For example, in financial time series, the impact of seasonality might be proportional to the level of the data.

Decomposition Using Python

Python provides various libraries for time series decomposition. One commonly used library is statsmodels. Here's a step-by-step guide on how to perform time series decomposition using statsmodels:

1. **Import the Necessary Libraries**:

```python
import pandas as pd
import statsmodels.api as sm
import matplotlib.pyplot as plt
```

2. **Load the Time Series Data**:

```python
# Load your time series data into a pandas DataFrame with a datetime in
dex.
# For example, if your data has two columns 'date' and 'value':
df = pd.read_csv('your_time_series_data.csv')
df['date'] = pd.to_datetime(df['date'])
df.set_index('date', inplace=True)
```

3. **Perform Decomposition**:

```python
decomposition = sm.tsa.seasonal_decompose(df['value'], model='additive'
)
```

4. **Visualize the Components**:

```python
fig, (ax1, ax2, ax3, ax4) = plt.subplots(4, 1, figsize=(12, 8))
decomposition.observed.plot(ax=ax1)
ax1.set_ylabel('Observed')
decomposition.trend.plot(ax=ax2)
ax2.set_ylabel('Trend')
decomposition.seasonal.plot(ax=ax3)
ax3.set_ylabel('Seasonal')
decomposition.resid.plot(ax=ax4)
```

```
ax4.set_ylabel('Residuals')
plt.tight_layout()
plt.show()
```

This code will produce a set of subplots displaying the observed time series, trend, seasonal component, and residuals. Analyzing these components can provide valuable insights into the underlying patterns and behavior of the time series data, which is essential for making informed decisions and forecasting future values.

In the subsequent sections, we will explore more advanced time series forecasting methods and techniques to make predictions based on the insights gained from decomposition.

Section 12.3: ARIMA Models for Time Series Forecasting

Autoregressive Integrated Moving Average (ARIMA) models are widely used for time series forecasting. They are a class of models that capture different aspects of time series data, including autocorrelation, seasonality, and trend. In this section, we'll explore ARIMA models, understand their components, and learn how to build them using Python.

Components of ARIMA Models

ARIMA models consist of three main components:

1. **AutoRegressive (AR) Component**: The AR component captures the relationship between the current value and previous values in the time series. It accounts for autocorrelation, where the current value depends on its own past values. The order of the AR component, denoted as p, represents the number of lag observations included in the model.

2. **Integrated (I) Component**: The I component represents the number of differences needed to make the time series stationary. Stationarity is an important property for ARIMA models, as they assume that the data is stationary. If the data is not stationary (i.e., it has a trend or seasonality), differencing is performed until stationarity is achieved. The order of differencing, denoted as d, represents the number of differences applied to the data.

3. **Moving Average (MA) Component**: The MA component models the relationship between the current value and past white noise or error terms. It accounts for the residual errors from the autoregressive part. The order of the MA component, denoted as q, represents the number of lagged forecast errors included in the model.

Building ARIMA Models in Python

To build an ARIMA model in Python, you can use the `statsmodels` library. Here's a step-by-step guide:

1. **Import the Necessary Libraries**:

```
import pandas as pd
import numpy as np
import statsmodels.api as sm
import matplotlib.pyplot as plt
```

2. **Load and Prepare the Time Series Data**:

```
# Load your time series data into a pandas DataFrame with a datetime in
dex.
# For example, if your data has two columns 'date' and 'value':
df = pd.read_csv('your_time_series_data.csv')
df['date'] = pd.to_datetime(df['date'])
df.set_index('date', inplace=True)

# Ensure that the data is stationary by differencing if needed.
df['stationary_data'] = df['value'].diff(periods=1)
```

3. **Choose ARIMA Orders**:

   Determine the values of p, d, and q for your ARIMA model. You can use techniques like autocorrelation and partial autocorrelation plots to help with this selection.

4. **Build and Fit the ARIMA Model**:

```
p, d, q = 1, 1, 1   # Replace with your chosen values
model = sm.tsa.ARIMA(df['stationary_data'].dropna(), order=(p, d, q))
results = model.fit()
```

5. **Visualize the Model's Performance**:

```
# Plot the original time series and the model's predictions.
plt.figure(figsize=(12, 6))
plt.plot(df['value'], label='Original Data')
plt.plot(results.fittedvalues, color='red', label='ARIMA Model')
plt.legend()
plt.xlabel('Date')
plt.ylabel('Value')
plt.title('ARIMA Model Forecast')
plt.show()
```

This code will fit an ARIMA model to your time series data and plot the original data alongside the model's predictions. You can evaluate the model's performance using appropriate metrics, such as mean squared error (MSE) or root mean squared error (RMSE).

ARIMA models are powerful tools for time series forecasting, but they may require fine-tuning of hyperparameters and additional diagnostics to ensure that they provide accurate predictions. In practice, you may also explore more advanced time series forecasting methods, such as SARIMA or Prophet, for improved performance on specific types of time series data.

Section 12.4: Prophet for Time Series Forecasting

Prophet is an open-source forecasting tool developed by Facebook's Core Data Science team. It is designed to make time series forecasting accessible to non-experts while providing advanced capabilities for experienced forecasters. In this section, we'll explore Prophet and learn how to use it for time series forecasting in Python.

Key Features of Prophet

Prophet offers several key features that make it a popular choice for time series forecasting:

1. **Automatic Seasonality Detection**: Prophet can automatically detect yearly, weekly, and daily seasonality in your time series data. This is especially useful for datasets with complex seasonal patterns.

2. **Holiday Effects**: It allows you to include holidays and special events as additional components in your forecasting model. You can specify the holidays relevant to your dataset, and Prophet will consider their impact on the forecasts.

3. **Trend Forecasting**: Prophet can model both linear and non-linear trends in the data. It provides flexibility in capturing trend patterns that change over time.

4. **Handling Missing Data**: Prophet handles missing data gracefully and imputes them as part of the forecasting process, making it robust to data quality issues.

5. **Custom Seasonality**: You can define custom seasonalities if your data exhibits patterns that are not captured by the automatic seasonality detection.

6. **Forecast Uncertainty**: Prophet provides uncertainty intervals around the forecasted values, giving you insights into the range of possible outcomes.

Building Prophet Models in Python

To use Prophet for time series forecasting in Python, you'll need to follow these steps:

1. **Install the Prophet Library**:

   You can install Prophet using pip:

   ```
   pip install fbprophet
   ```

2. **Import Libraries and Prepare Data**:

   ```
   import pandas as pd
   from fbprophet import Prophet

   # Load your time series data into a pandas DataFrame with two columns:
   'ds' (datetime) and 'y' (value).
   ```

```
df = pd.read_csv('your_time_series_data.csv')
df['ds'] = pd.to_datetime(df['ds'])
```

3. **Create and Fit the Prophet Model**:

```
# Create a Prophet model.
model = Prophet()

# Fit the model to your data.
model.fit(df)
```

4. **Generate Future Data Points**:

To make forecasts, you need to create a DataFrame with future dates. Prophet provides the make_future_dataframe method for this purpose:

```
future = model.make_future_dataframe(periods=365)  # Forecasting for 1
year into the future
```

5. **Make Forecasts**:

```
# Generate forecasts for the future dates.
forecast = model.predict(future)
```

6. **Visualize Forecasts**:

Prophet includes built-in plotting capabilities to visualize the forecasts:

```
fig = model.plot(forecast)
```

Prophet's forecasting results will include predictions, trend components, seasonal components, and uncertainty intervals.

Prophet is a versatile tool that can handle a wide range of time series forecasting tasks. It's particularly useful for datasets with multiple seasonalities and holidays, making it a valuable addition to the toolkit of data scientists and analysts working with time series data.

Section 12.5: Evaluating Time Series Models

Evaluating time series forecasting models is crucial to assess their performance and reliability. In this section, we'll explore various techniques and metrics for evaluating the effectiveness of your time series models.

Key Metrics for Time Series Evaluation

1. Mean Absolute Error (MAE):

MAE measures the average absolute errors between predicted and actual values. It provides a simple and interpretable measure of forecasting accuracy. Lower MAE values indicate better performance.

```python
from sklearn.metrics import mean_absolute_error

mae = mean_absolute_error(actual_values, predicted_values)
```

2. Mean Squared Error (MSE):

MSE measures the average squared errors between predicted and actual values. It penalizes larger errors more heavily. Like MAE, lower MSE values indicate better accuracy.

```python
from sklearn.metrics import mean_squared_error

mse = mean_squared_error(actual_values, predicted_values)
```

3. Root Mean Squared Error (RMSE):

RMSE is the square root of MSE. It's in the same unit as the target variable, making it more interpretable. RMSE values closer to zero are preferred.

```python
import numpy as np

rmse = np.sqrt(mean_squared_error(actual_values, predicted_values))
```

4. Mean Absolute Percentage Error (MAPE):

MAPE expresses errors as a percentage of actual values. It's useful for understanding the relative error. Lower MAPE values are better.

```python
def mean_absolute_percentage_error(y_true, y_pred):
    return np.mean(np.abs((y_true - y_pred) / y_true)) * 100

mape = mean_absolute_percentage_error(actual_values, predicted_values)
```

5. Forecast Bias:

Forecast bias measures the average overestimation or underestimation of the forecasts. A bias near zero indicates balanced forecasts.

```python
bias = np.mean(predicted_values - actual_values)
```

Cross-Validation for Time Series

When working with time series data, simple train-test splits may not provide an accurate assessment of model performance. Time series cross-validation, such as **TimeSeriesSplit** in scikit-learn, is more suitable. It creates multiple training and testing sets by gradually moving the training window through the time series.

```python
from sklearn.model_selection import TimeSeriesSplit

tscv = TimeSeriesSplit(n_splits=5)
for train_index, test_index in tscv.split(data):
    train_data, test_data = data[train_index], data[test_index]
    # Fit and evaluate the model on train_data and test_data
```

Visualizing Forecasts

Visualization is essential for understanding how well your time series model captures the data's patterns and trends. Time series plots, like line charts with actual and predicted values, can reveal discrepancies and provide insights into model behavior.

Remember that the choice of evaluation metrics depends on your specific forecasting problem and business requirements. It's often advisable to use a combination of metrics to gain a comprehensive understanding of your model's performance.

Chapter 13: Reinforcement Learning

Section 13.1: Introduction to Reinforcement Learning

Reinforcement Learning (RL) is a subfield of machine learning that focuses on training agents to make sequences of decisions in an environment to maximize cumulative rewards. Unlike supervised learning, where the model is trained on labeled data, RL operates in an interactive setting where the agent learns by trial and error.

Key Concepts in Reinforcement Learning

1. Agent:

The learner or decision-maker that interacts with the environment.

2. Environment:

The external system with which the agent interacts and learns from. It includes everything the agent doesn't control but can sense and react to.

3. State (S):

A representation of the environment at a given time. It captures all relevant information for decision-making.

4. Action (A):

The set of possible moves or decisions that the agent can make.

5. Policy (π):

A strategy that the agent follows to select actions based on states. It defines the mapping from states to actions.

6. Reward (R):

A numerical value that the environment provides to the agent after each action. The agent's objective is to maximize cumulative rewards.

7. Episode:

A single run of the agent interacting with the environment from start to finish. Episodes are often used for learning and evaluation.

8. Value Function (V):

The expected cumulative reward an agent can obtain from a given state or state-action pair. It helps the agent assess the desirability of states or actions.

The expected cumulative reward an agent can obtain starting from a state, taking a specific action, and following a particular policy.

Reinforcement Learning Workflow

The typical RL workflow consists of the following steps:

1. **Initialization**:
   - Define the agent, environment, state space, action space, and rewards.
   - Initialize the agent's policy, value function, or Q-function.

2. **Interaction**:
   - The agent takes actions in the environment based on its current policy.
   - The environment provides feedback in the form of rewards.

3. **Learning**:
   - The agent updates its policy, value function, or Q-function based on the received rewards and its observations.
   - Common algorithms include Q-Learning, Deep Q-Networks (DQN), Policy Gradients, and more.

4. **Evaluation**:
   - Assess the agent's performance using metrics like the total reward accumulated over episodes.

5. **Deployment**:
   - Deploy the trained RL agent in a real-world or simulated environment to make decisions.

Applications of Reinforcement Learning

Reinforcement Learning has found applications in various domains:

- **Game Playing**: RL has achieved superhuman performance in games like Go and chess.

- **Robotics**: RL is used for robot control, autonomous navigation, and grasping objects.

- **Finance**: RL is applied to portfolio optimization, trading strategies, and risk management.

- **Healthcare**: RL aids in personalized treatment plans and resource allocation in healthcare.

- **Autonomous Vehicles**: RL is crucial for autonomous cars and drones.

- **Recommendation Systems**: RL can be used for personalized content recommendations.

- **Natural Language Processing**: RL powers chatbots and dialogue systems.

- **Industrial Control**: RL helps optimize manufacturing processes and supply chain management.

Reinforcement Learning is a dynamic and evolving field with ongoing research, making it an exciting area for both learning and practical applications. In the sections that follow, we will delve into specific RL algorithms and their real-world applications.

Section 13.2: Q-Learning

Q-Learning is a fundamental reinforcement learning algorithm used for solving Markov Decision Processes (MDPs). It's a model-free, value-based method that aims to learn the optimal action-selection policy for an agent to maximize its expected cumulative reward over time.

Key Concepts in Q-Learning

1. Q-Table:

At the heart of Q-Learning is the Q-table, which stores the estimated values (Q-values) for state-action pairs. Each entry in the table represents the expected cumulative reward of taking a particular action in a specific state.

2. Bellman Equation:

Q-Learning updates the Q-values iteratively using the Bellman equation:

$Q(s, a) = Q(s, a) + \alpha * [R + \gamma * max(Q(s', a')) - Q(s, a)]$

- $Q(s, a)$: Q-value for state-action pair (s, a).
- α (alpha): Learning rate, controlling the step size in value updates.
- R: Immediate reward received after taking action a in state s.
- γ (gamma): Discount factor, representing the importance of future rewards.
- $max(Q(s', a'))$: The maximum Q-value among possible actions in the next state s'.

3. Exploration vs. Exploitation:

Q-Learning balances exploration (trying new actions to discover better ones) and exploitation (selecting the best-known action) using an exploration strategy. The ε-greedy strategy is common, where the agent selects the best action with probability 1 - ε and a random action with probability ε.

Q-Learning Algorithm

1. **Initialize Q-Table**: Create a Q-table with all Q-values initially set to arbitrary values.

2. **Select Action**: Choose an action using the ε-greedy strategy based on the current Q-table and exploration rate.

3. **Take Action**: Execute the selected action in the environment and observe the next state and the reward.

4. **Update Q-Value**: Update the Q-value for the current state-action pair using the Bellman equation.

5. **Repeat**: Continue selecting actions, taking actions, and updating Q-values iteratively until convergence or a maximum number of episodes.

6. **Convergence**: Q-Learning often converges to the optimal Q-values under certain conditions, ensuring the agent's policy becomes optimal.

Pseudocode

Here's a simplified pseudocode for Q-Learning:

```
Initialize Q-table Q(s, a) arbitrarily
Repeat for each episode:
    Initialize the state (s)
    Repeat for each step or until the goal is reached:
        Choose action (a) using ε-greedy policy based on Q(s, a)
        Take action (a) and observe reward (R) and the next state (s')
        Update Q(s, a) using the Bellman equation
        Set the current state to the next state (s <- s')
    Until the goal is reached or a maximum number of steps
```

Applications of Q-Learning

Q-Learning has been applied to various tasks, including:

- **Game Playing**: It has been used to develop agents that learn to play games like Tic-Tac-Toe, chess, and more.

- **Robotics**: Q-Learning helps robots learn navigation and control policies in real-world environments.

- **Autonomous Vehicles**: It plays a role in self-driving car decision-making.

- **Resource Allocation**: Q-Learning can optimize resource allocation in networking and cloud computing.

- **Inventory Management**: It aids in inventory control and supply chain optimization.

- **Energy Management**: Q-Learning optimizes energy consumption in smart grids and buildings.

In the next section, we will explore Deep Q-Networks (DQN), which extends Q-Learning to handle high-dimensional state spaces using neural networks.

Section 13.3: Deep Q-Networks (DQN)

Deep Q-Networks (DQN) is an extension of Q-Learning that addresses the limitations of traditional Q-Learning when dealing with high-dimensional state spaces, such as those encountered in many real-world applications. DQN combines reinforcement learning with deep neural networks to approximate the Q-values, making it suitable for tasks like playing video games, robotic control, and more.

Key Concepts in Deep Q-Networks

1. *Neural Networks:*

DQN uses a deep neural network as a function approximator to estimate Q-values. The neural network takes the state as input and outputs Q-values for all possible actions. This network is often referred to as the Q-network.

2. *Experience Replay:*

To improve stability and data efficiency, DQN employs experience replay. It stores a replay buffer of past experiences (state, action, reward, next state) and samples mini-batches during training. This reduces the impact of correlated experiences and helps in learning from past interactions.

3. *Target Network:*

DQN introduces the concept of a target network, which is a copy of the Q-network. The target network is used to stabilize training by providing fixed Q-value targets for the Q-network. The target network is periodically updated to match the Q-network's weights.

4. *Loss Function:*

The loss function for training the Q-network is typically the mean squared error (MSE) loss between the predicted Q-values and the target Q-values. The target Q-values are computed using the Bellman equation with the target network.

5. *Epsilon-Greedy Policy:*

DQN often employs an epsilon-greedy policy for exploration, similar to Q-Learning. The agent selects the best-known action with high probability $(1 - \varepsilon)$ and a random action with low probability (ε).

DQN Algorithm
1. **Initialize Q-Network and Target Network**: Create two neural networks - the Q-network and the target network, with the same architecture but different weights.

2. **Initialize Replay Buffer**: Create an empty replay buffer to store past experiences.

3. **Select Action**: Choose an action using the epsilon-greedy policy based on the Q-network.

4. **Take Action**: Execute the selected action in the environment and observe the reward and the next state.

5. **Store Experience**: Add the experience (state, action, reward, next state) to the replay buffer.

6. **Sample Mini-Batch**: Periodically sample a mini-batch of experiences from the replay buffer.

7. **Calculate Target Q-Values**: Use the target network to calculate the target Q-values for the mini-batch using the Bellman equation.

8. **Update Q-Network**: Update the Q-network's weights by minimizing the MSE loss between predicted and target Q-values.

9. **Periodic Target Network Update**: Periodically update the target network's weights to match the Q-network.

10. **Repeat**: Continue selecting actions, taking actions, and updating networks iteratively until convergence or a maximum number of episodes.

Pseudocode

Here's a simplified pseudocode for Deep Q-Networks:

```
Initialize Q-network and target network with random weights
Initialize replay buffer
Repeat for each episode:
    Initialize the state (s)
    Repeat for each step or until the goal is reached:
        Choose action (a) using epsilon-greedy policy based on Q-network
        Take action (a) and observe reward (R) and the next state (s')
        Store experience (s, a, R, s') in the replay buffer
        Sample mini-batch of experiences from replay buffer
        Calculate target Q-values using the target network
        Update Q-network's weights by minimizing MSE loss
        Periodically update target network's weights to match Q-network
        Set the current state to the next state (s <- s')
    Until the goal is reached or a maximum number of steps
```

Applications of DQN

DQN has achieved remarkable success in various domains:

- **Atari Games**: DQN became famous for its ability to play a wide range of Atari 2600 games at a superhuman level.

- **Robotics**: DQN has been used for robot control, enabling robots to learn tasks like grasping objects and navigation.

- **Autonomous Vehicles**: It plays a role in self-driving car decision-making and control.

- **Recommendation Systems**: DQN has been applied to personalized recommendation systems.

- **Finance**: DQN can optimize trading strategies and portfolio management.

In the next section, we will explore policy gradients, another class of reinforcement learning algorithms that directly learn a policy for actions.

Section 13.4: Policy Gradients

Policy gradient methods are a class of reinforcement learning algorithms that focus on directly learning a policy, which is a mapping from states to actions, rather than estimating value functions like Q-learning or DQN. These methods are particularly useful when dealing with high-dimensional action spaces or continuous action spaces.

Key Concepts in Policy Gradients

1. Policy Function:

In policy gradient methods, we parameterize the policy using a function approximator, often a neural network. The policy function takes the current state as input and outputs a probability distribution over possible actions.

2. Policy Gradient:

The objective in policy gradient methods is to maximize the expected cumulative reward. This is done by adjusting the parameters of the policy function to increase the probability of good actions and decrease the probability of bad actions. Policy gradients provide a principled way to compute these parameter updates.

3. Reward Signal:

The reward signal is a scalar value received from the environment after taking an action in a given state. In policy gradients, we use the reward signal to estimate the quality of actions and update the policy accordingly.

4. Policy Update Rule:

The policy update rule in policy gradient methods is often based on the gradient of the expected return with respect to the policy parameters. The objective is to find parameter updates that increase the likelihood of actions that led to higher rewards.

Policy gradient methods typically use stochastic policies, where actions are sampled from a probability distribution. This introduces exploration and allows the policy to balance between exploration and exploitation.

6. *Actor-Critic Methods:*

Actor-critic methods combine policy gradient with value function estimation. The actor (policy) is updated using policy gradients, while the critic (value function) estimates the expected return and provides a baseline for policy updates.

Policy Gradient Algorithm

The general steps of a policy gradient algorithm are as follows:

1. **Initialize Policy**: Initialize the policy function with random parameters or pre-trained weights.

2. **Collect Trajectories**: Interact with the environment to collect trajectories by following the current policy. Store the states, actions, and rewards encountered.

3. **Compute Returns**: Calculate the returns (cumulative rewards) for each time step in the trajectories. This can involve discounting future rewards.

4. **Compute Gradients**: Compute the gradient of the expected return with respect to the policy parameters. This involves estimating the gradient using the collected trajectories and the returns.

5. **Update Policy**: Update the policy parameters in the direction that maximizes expected return. This can be done using gradient ascent.

6. **Repeat**: Repeat the above steps for multiple iterations or until convergence.

Advantages of Policy Gradients

- Policy gradients are suitable for problems with high-dimensional or continuous action spaces.

- They can learn stochastic policies, which helps in exploration.

- Policy gradients have been successful in tasks like robotics, natural language processing, and games.

Challenges of Policy Gradients

- Policy gradient methods can have high variance in the gradient estimates, which can lead to slow convergence.

- Determining good hyperparameters can be challenging.

- The sample efficiency of policy gradient methods may be lower compared to some value-based methods.

In the next section, we will explore real-world applications and case studies of reinforcement learning, including those that use policy gradients.

Section 13.5: Real-World Applications of Reinforcement Learning

Reinforcement learning (RL) has found application in various domains, and its real-world impact continues to grow. In this section, we will explore some notable applications of RL in diverse fields.

1. Game Playing:

RL algorithms have achieved remarkable success in playing complex games. AlphaGo, developed by DeepMind, defeated the world champion Go player using RL techniques. Similarly, OpenAI's Dota 2-playing AI, OpenAI Five, demonstrated RL's capability in strategic games.

2. Robotics:

Reinforcement learning plays a crucial role in robotics, enabling robots to learn tasks through trial and error. RL has been used for robot control, manipulation, and navigation in both simulated and real-world environments.

3. Autonomous Vehicles:

RL is applied in autonomous driving to teach vehicles how to make driving decisions based on sensory input. It helps in handling complex traffic scenarios and ensures safe navigation.

4. Healthcare:

RL has applications in personalized treatment planning and medical diagnosis. RL algorithms can optimize treatment plans for individual patients based on their responses to different therapies.

5. Finance:

In finance, RL is used for algorithmic trading, portfolio optimization, and fraud detection. Traders employ RL to make real-time decisions in dynamic markets.

6. Recommendation Systems:

Online platforms use RL to create recommendation systems that suggest products, movies, or content to users based on their preferences and past interactions.

7. Natural Language Processing (NLP):

RL techniques are applied to train chatbots and virtual assistants, enabling them to engage in meaningful conversations and provide relevant responses.

8. Supply Chain Management:

Reinforcement learning can optimize inventory management, logistics, and supply chain operations, leading to cost savings and efficiency improvements.

9. Energy Management:

RL is employed to optimize energy consumption in smart grids and industrial processes, reducing energy costs and environmental impact.

10. Game Development:

Game developers use RL to create non-player characters (NPCs) with adaptive behaviors, enhancing the gaming experience.

Challenges and Future Directions:

Despite the successes, RL faces challenges such as sample efficiency, safety concerns, and the need for explainable AI. Future research may focus on addressing these challenges and expanding RL's applications in various domains.

In conclusion, reinforcement learning has evolved from a theoretical concept to a practical tool with wide-ranging applications. Its ability to learn from interaction and adapt to dynamic environments makes it a valuable technology in fields where decision-making and optimization are essential. As RL continues to advance, it holds promise for solving complex real-world problems and driving innovation across industries.

Chapter 14: Model Deployment and Serving

Section 14.1: Exporting Machine Learning Models

Once you've trained a machine learning model, the next crucial step is deploying it to make predictions on new data. Model deployment involves making your model accessible for use by applications, websites, or other systems. In this section, we will discuss the initial steps of deploying a machine learning model: exporting and saving the model in a format that can be easily loaded and used in various environments.

Why Exporting Matters

Exporting a machine learning model is essential because it allows you to separate the training and deployment phases. During training, you build and optimize the model using historical data. After training, you export the model, which can then be loaded and used by other processes or services. This separation of concerns is crucial for scalability, maintainability, and collaboration.

Common Model Export Formats

Machine learning frameworks provide tools and libraries to export models in various formats. Some of the common export formats include:

1. **Serialized Models**: Many machine learning libraries support saving models in their serialized form. For example, in Python, you can use the `joblib` library to serialize Scikit-learn models or `pickle` for generic Python objects. Serialized models are easy to save and load but may be library-specific.

2. **HDF5 (Hierarchical Data Format)**: HDF5 is a file format that is commonly used for saving large datasets, but it's also suitable for saving deep learning models. Frameworks like TensorFlow and Keras allow you to save models in HDF5 format.

3. **ONNX (Open Neural Network Exchange)**: ONNX is an open format for representing machine learning models. It's designed to be interoperable across different frameworks. You can export models to ONNX format using tools provided by various libraries.

4. **PMML (Predictive Model Markup Language)**: PMML is an XML-based standard for representing predictive models. It's particularly useful for exporting models from certain data mining and analytics tools.

Exporting a Model in Python

The process of exporting a model in Python depends on the library or framework you're using. Here's a high-level example of exporting a Scikit-learn model:

```
import joblib

# Train your Scikit-learn model (e.g., a RandomForestClassifier)
model = RandomForestClassifier()
model.fit(X_train, y_train)

# Export the model to a file
joblib.dump(model, 'model.joblib')
```

And here's an example of exporting a TensorFlow/Keras model to HDF5 format:

```
from tensorflow.keras.models import Sequential
from tensorflow.keras.layers import Dense

# Create a simple Keras model
model = Sequential([
    Dense(64, activation='relu', input_shape=(input_dim,)),
    Dense(32, activation='relu'),
    Dense(output_dim, activation='softmax')
])

# Compile and train the model
model.compile(optimizer='adam', loss='categorical_crossentropy', metrics=['ac
curacy'])
model.fit(X_train, y_train, epochs=10)

# Export the model to HDF5 format
model.save('model.h5')
```

These are just basic examples, and the exact process may vary depending on your specific use case and the machine learning library you're using. Additionally, when deploying models to production, you'll need to consider versioning, monitoring, and serving the model via APIs, which will be covered in subsequent sections of this chapter.

Section 14.2: Building RESTful APIs with Flask

Building a RESTful API is a common way to serve machine learning models for predictions in a production environment. In this section, we'll explore how to create a simple RESTful API using Flask, a lightweight web framework in Python.

Why Use Flask for API Development

Flask is a micro web framework that is ideal for creating web applications, including APIs. It is minimalistic and provides just the essentials needed for building web applications, making it easy to learn and use. Flask is also highly extensible, allowing you to add libraries and components as needed for your specific project. These characteristics make it a popular choice for building RESTful APIs.

Setting Up Flask

Before creating a RESTful API with Flask, you need to install Flask using pip:

```
pip install Flask
```

Once Flask is installed, you can create a Python script for your API. Here's a simple example of setting up a Flask app:

```python
from flask import Flask

app = Flask(__name__)

@app.route('/')
def hello_world():
    return 'Hello, World!'

if __name__ == '__main__':
    app.run()
```

In this example, we've created a basic Flask app with a single route that returns "Hello, World!" when you access the root URL.

Creating an API Endpoint for Model Prediction

To serve machine learning model predictions, you'll need to create a new route in your Flask app. Here's an example of how you can add a route for making predictions using a Scikit-learn model:

```python
from flask import Flask, request, jsonify
import joblib

app = Flask(__name__)

# Load the pre-trained Scikit-learn model
model = joblib.load('model.joblib')

@app.route('/predict', methods=['POST'])
def predict():
    try:
        # Get input data as JSON
        data = request.get_json()

        # Perform prediction using the loaded model
        prediction = model.predict(data['features'])

        # Return the prediction as JSON
        return jsonify({'prediction': prediction.tolist()})
    except Exception as e:
        return jsonify({'error': str(e)})
```

```
if __name__ == '__main__':
    app.run()
```

In this code, we've added a new route /predict that accepts POST requests with input data in JSON format. It loads the pre-trained Scikit-learn model and uses it to make predictions based on the input data. The predictions are returned as JSON.

Running the Flask API

To run the Flask API, simply execute your Python script. By default, the Flask development server will run on http://localhost:5000/. You can access your API using tools like curl, Postman, or by creating client applications that send HTTP requests to the API endpoints.

This is a basic example of how to create a RESTful API with Flask for serving machine learning models. In practice, you'll want to add more features like input validation, error handling, and possibly authentication depending on your project's requirements.

Section 14.3: Containerization with Docker

Containerization is a technology that allows you to package an application and its dependencies together into a single container. Docker is one of the most popular containerization platforms, and it can be a valuable tool for deploying machine learning models and RESTful APIs in a consistent and reproducible manner.

Why Use Docker for Model Deployment

Docker containers provide a way to encapsulate your machine learning models and their runtime environments. Here are some reasons why Docker is useful for model deployment:

1. **Isolation**: Containers isolate applications and their dependencies from the host system. This ensures that your model runs consistently across different environments.

2. **Reproducibility**: Docker containers make it easy to reproduce the exact environment in which your model was trained and tested, reducing the "it works on my machine" problem.

3. **Scalability**: Docker containers can be easily scaled up or down to handle varying levels of traffic and load.

4. **Portability**: Docker containers can run on any system that supports Docker, making it easy to deploy your model in different environments, including cloud platforms.

Creating a Dockerfile

To containerize your machine learning model and API, you need to create a Dockerfile. A Dockerfile is a text file that contains instructions for building a Docker image. Here's a basic example of a Dockerfile for a Flask-based machine learning API:

```
# Use an official Python runtime as a parent image
FROM python:3.8-slim

# Set the working directory to /app
WORKDIR /app

# Copy the current directory contents into the container at /app
COPY . /app

# Install any needed packages specified in requirements.txt
RUN pip install --trusted-host pypi.python.org -r requirements.txt

# Make port 80 available to the world outside this container
EXPOSE 80

# Define environment variable
ENV NAME World

# Run app.py when the container launches
CMD ["python", "app.py"]
```

In this example, we start with an official Python 3.8 image, set the working directory to /app, copy the application code and dependencies, expose port 80, set an environment variable, and define the command to run when the container launches.

Building and Running the Docker Container

To build a Docker container using the Dockerfile, navigate to the directory containing the Dockerfile and run the following command:

```
docker build -t my-ml-api .
```

This command builds a Docker image named my-ml-api from the current directory (.).

Once the image is built, you can run a container based on that image with the following command:

```
docker run -p 4000:80 my-ml-api
```

This command maps port 4000 on your host machine to port 80 inside the container, allowing you to access your API from http://localhost:4000.

Deploying to the Cloud with Docker

Docker makes it straightforward to deploy your containerized machine learning models and APIs to cloud platforms such as Amazon Web Services (AWS), Google Cloud Platform (GCP), or Microsoft Azure. Each cloud provider has its own container orchestration services (e.g., AWS Elastic Kubernetes Service, GCP Kubernetes Engine) that can help you manage and scale your Docker containers in the cloud.

Containerization with Docker simplifies the process of packaging, deploying, and scaling machine learning models, making it a valuable tool for production deployment.

Section 14.4: Cloud Deployment (AWS, Azure, GCP)

Deploying machine learning models and applications in the cloud offers scalability, reliability, and accessibility benefits. This section will explore cloud deployment options using three major cloud providers: Amazon Web Services (AWS), Microsoft Azure, and Google Cloud Platform (GCP).

AWS Deployment

Amazon Web Services (AWS) provides a wide range of services for deploying machine learning models and applications. Some of the key AWS services for ML deployment include:

1. **Amazon SageMaker**: SageMaker is a fully managed service that simplifies the process of building, training, and deploying machine learning models at scale. It supports various ML frameworks and provides a Jupyter Notebook interface for model development.

2. **AWS Lambda**: Lambda allows you to run code in response to events and triggers. You can use it to create serverless APIs and deploy machine learning models as microservices.

3. **Amazon Elastic Container Service (ECS)**: ECS enables you to deploy Docker containers at scale. You can containerize your ML applications and manage them using ECS.

4. **AWS Elastic Beanstalk**: Elastic Beanstalk is a Platform-as-a-Service (PaaS) offering that makes it easy to deploy and manage web applications and services, including machine learning APIs.

Azure Deployment

Microsoft Azure offers several services and tools for deploying machine learning models:

1. **Azure Machine Learning**: Azure ML is a cloud-based service for building, training, and deploying machine learning models. It provides a drag-and-drop interface for model creation and supports various ML frameworks.

2. **Azure Functions**: Azure Functions is a serverless compute service that allows you to run event-driven code, making it suitable for deploying ML models as APIs.

3. **Azure Kubernetes Service (AKS)**: AKS is a managed Kubernetes container orchestration service. You can deploy containerized ML applications and scale them using AKS.

4. **Azure App Service**: App Service is a PaaS offering that simplifies web app deployment. You can deploy ML-powered web applications and APIs with ease.

GCP Deployment

Google Cloud Platform (GCP) offers a range of services for deploying machine learning models:

1. **Google Cloud AI Platform**: AI Platform provides a managed environment for building and deploying ML models. It supports TensorFlow and scikit-learn, among other frameworks.

2. **Google Cloud Functions**: Cloud Functions is GCP's serverless compute service. You can deploy ML model inference code as functions that respond to HTTP requests.

3. **Google Kubernetes Engine (GKE)**: GKE is a managed Kubernetes service. It's suitable for deploying containerized ML applications that require scaling and orchestration.

4. **Google App Engine**: App Engine is a PaaS offering that allows you to deploy web applications and services, including those powered by machine learning models.

Choosing the Right Cloud Provider

The choice of cloud provider depends on your specific requirements, familiarity with the platform, and any existing cloud partnerships your organization may have. Each cloud provider offers unique features and pricing structures, so it's essential to evaluate them carefully before making a decision.

Before deploying your ML model to the cloud, consider factors like data storage, scalability, security, and cost. Additionally, most cloud providers offer free tiers or trial credits, allowing you to experiment and determine which platform best meets your needs.

In conclusion, cloud deployment offers a powerful way to make your machine learning models and applications accessible to a broader audience while benefiting from cloud providers' infrastructure and services. Choose the cloud provider that aligns with your project's requirements and leverage their tools to simplify the deployment process.

Section 14.5: Monitoring and Scaling Models in Production

Once you've deployed your machine learning models to a production environment, your work is far from over. Monitoring and scaling are crucial aspects of maintaining a successful machine learning system. This section explores best practices for monitoring the performance of your deployed models and strategies for scaling them as needed.

Monitoring Machine Learning Models

1. **Performance Metrics**: Continuously monitor key performance metrics for your models. These metrics might include accuracy, precision, recall, F1-score, and more, depending on the problem type (classification, regression, etc.).

2. **Data Drift Detection**: Set up data drift detection to identify changes in the distribution of incoming data. Sudden shifts in data characteristics can degrade model performance.

3. **Model Drift Detection**: Monitor for model drift, which occurs when a model's predictions degrade over time due to changes in the underlying data patterns. Implement automated retraining if drift is detected.

4. **Latency and Throughput**: Keep an eye on the latency (response time) and throughput (requests per second) of your model's API. Ensure that it meets service-level objectives (SLOs).

5. **Resource Utilization**: Monitor the utilization of computational resources (CPU, memory, GPU, etc.) to optimize cost and performance. Auto-scaling can be used to adjust resources as needed.

6. **Error Tracking**: Implement error tracking to log and analyze errors or exceptions that occur during model inference. Rapid identification and resolution of issues are essential.

7. **Security and Privacy**: Regularly assess and update security measures to protect your models and data. Ensure compliance with privacy regulations, especially for sensitive data.

Scaling Machine Learning Models

1. **Vertical Scaling**: Increase the computational power of your deployment infrastructure by adding more CPU, memory, or GPU resources to a single server. Vertical scaling is suitable for handling increased loads up to a point.

2. **Horizontal Scaling**: Distribute incoming requests across multiple server instances to handle high traffic. Load balancers are commonly used for distributing requests evenly.

3. **Containerization**: Use containerization technologies like Docker to package your model and its dependencies. Container orchestration platforms like Kubernetes can help manage and scale containers efficiently.

4. **Serverless Computing**: Consider serverless platforms (e.g., AWS Lambda, Azure Functions, Google Cloud Functions) for highly scalable and cost-effective deployments. Serverless automatically manages resource allocation.

5. **Auto-Scaling**: Implement auto-scaling policies based on traffic or resource utilization. Cloud providers offer auto-scaling solutions that automatically adjust the number of server instances.

6. **Caching**: Implement caching mechanisms for frequently requested data or model predictions. Caching can significantly reduce the load on your model-serving infrastructure.

*7. **Content Delivery Networks (CDNs)**: Use CDNs to cache and serve static assets (e.g., model artifacts, images) closer to end-users, reducing latency and load on your infrastructure.*

Continuous Improvement

Continuous improvement is key to maintaining high-performing machine learning models in production. Regularly review monitoring data, conduct root cause analysis for issues, and iterate on your models and deployment strategies. Keep your models up to date by retraining them with fresh data periodically, ensuring they remain relevant and accurate.

In summary, monitoring and scaling are integral parts of managing machine learning models in production. By establishing robust monitoring practices and implementing scalable deployment strategies, you can deliver reliable and performant machine learning services to your users while efficiently managing resources and costs.

Chapter 15: Ethics and Bias in Machine Learning

Section 15.1: Understanding Bias and Fairness

In the field of machine learning and artificial intelligence, it's critical to consider the ethical implications of the models we build and deploy. One of the key ethical considerations is bias and fairness in machine learning systems. Bias refers to the presence of systematic and unfair discrimination in the predictions and decisions made by a machine learning model. Fairness, on the other hand, relates to ensuring that these models treat all individuals or groups fairly and without discrimination.

What is Bias?

Bias in machine learning can manifest in various ways. It can be a result of biased training data, biased features, biased algorithms, or biased decision-making processes. Biased training data occurs when the data used to train a model is not representative of the real-world population, leading to skewed results. For example, if a facial recognition system is trained predominantly on data from one ethnicity, it may perform poorly for other ethnicities due to bias.

Types of Bias

There are several types of bias that can affect machine learning models:

1. *Selection Bias:*
   - **Example:** In healthcare, if electronic health records are used to train a model, it may exclude individuals who don't have access to healthcare, resulting in a selection bias.

2. *Sampling Bias:*
   - **Example:** When collecting survey data online, it may overrepresent certain demographics (e.g., tech-savvy individuals), leading to sampling bias.

3. *Measurement Bias:*
   - **Example:** If temperature measurements are taken using inaccurate sensors, it introduces measurement bias into climate prediction models.

4. *Algorithmic Bias:*
   - **Example:** Some machine learning algorithms may inherently favor certain outcomes or groups, leading to algorithmic bias.

Impact of Bias

Bias in machine learning models can have severe consequences. It can perpetuate and reinforce existing societal biases, lead to unfair treatment, and even violate anti-discrimination laws. In applications such as lending, hiring, and criminal justice, biased models can result in discrimination against certain groups.

Fairness in Machine Learning

Addressing bias and ensuring fairness in machine learning models is essential. Fairness measures aim to quantify and mitigate bias in model predictions. Some common fairness metrics include disparate impact, equal opportunity, and demographic parity. Techniques such as re-sampling, re-weighting, and adversarial training can be used to mitigate bias and improve fairness.

In the subsequent sections of this chapter, we will explore ethical considerations in machine learning, bias mitigation techniques, responsible AI development practices, and real-world case studies on ethical dilemmas. It's crucial for data scientists and machine learning practitioners to be aware of these issues and take proactive steps to build fair and unbiased models.

Section 15.2: Ethical Considerations in Machine Learning

Ethical considerations in machine learning encompass a wide range of topics, from data privacy and transparency to accountability and the potential societal impact of AI systems. As machine learning technologies become increasingly integrated into our daily lives, it's essential to address these ethical concerns to ensure responsible AI development.

Data Privacy

Protecting individuals' data privacy is a fundamental ethical principle. Machine learning models often require large amounts of data for training, and this data may contain sensitive information. It's crucial to implement robust data anonymization and encryption techniques to safeguard user privacy. Additionally, organizations must comply with data protection regulations, such as GDPR (General Data Protection Regulation) and HIPAA (Health Insurance Portability and Accountability Act), to avoid legal and ethical violations.

Transparency and Explainability

Understanding how machine learning models arrive at their decisions is crucial for transparency and accountability. Black-box models that provide no insight into their decision-making processes can be problematic, especially in high-stakes applications like healthcare and finance. Ethical AI development involves using interpretable models, providing explanations for predictions, and using techniques like LIME (Local Interpretable Model-agnostic Explanations) and SHAP (SHapley Additive exPlanations) to make models more understandable.

Accountability and Bias Mitigation

Machine learning practitioners and organizations must take responsibility for the ethical implications of their models. This includes identifying and mitigating biases in data and algorithms, as discussed in the previous section. Bias audits, continuous monitoring, and ethical guidelines can help ensure that models are accountable and fair. Additionally, establishing clear lines of responsibility within organizations for addressing ethical concerns is crucial.

Fairness and Non-Discrimination

Ensuring fairness and non-discrimination in machine learning models is paramount. AI systems should not discriminate against individuals or groups based on protected attributes such as race, gender, or age. To address this, fairness-aware machine learning techniques can be employed, and ethical guidelines should explicitly prohibit discriminatory practices.

Ethical Decision-Making

Developing ethical AI requires considering the broader societal impact of AI systems. When building AI applications, developers should assess potential risks and ethical dilemmas. This involves conducting impact assessments, soliciting public input, and engaging with interdisciplinary teams that include ethicists, social scientists, and domain experts. Ethical AI development should prioritize the well-being of society as a whole.

Case Studies on Ethical Dilemmas

Throughout this chapter, we will explore case studies that highlight real-world ethical dilemmas in machine learning. These case studies will shed light on the complex ethical considerations that arise in various domains, including healthcare, criminal justice, and autonomous vehicles. By examining these cases, we can better understand the challenges and responsibilities associated with AI technologies.

In conclusion, ethical considerations are at the core of responsible AI development. Practitioners and organizations must prioritize data privacy, transparency, fairness, and accountability to ensure that machine learning technologies benefit society while minimizing harm. Ethical AI is not only a moral imperative but also essential for building trust and maintaining the credibility of AI systems in the long term.

Section 15.3: Bias Mitigation Techniques

Bias in machine learning models is a significant ethical concern. Biased models can lead to unfair and discriminatory outcomes, perpetuating existing inequalities in society. It is crucial to address bias in both the data used to train machine learning models and the algorithms themselves. In this section, we will explore various techniques for mitigating bias in machine learning.

1. Data Preprocessing

a. Data Sampling

Data sampling techniques such as oversampling and undersampling can be used to balance the representation of different groups in the dataset. Oversampling minority groups and undersampling majority groups can help reduce bias in the training data.

b. Data Augmentation

Data augmentation involves generating synthetic data to balance the dataset. For image data, this can include techniques like rotating, flipping, or cropping images to create additional examples for underrepresented groups.

2. Algorithmic Techniques

a. Reweighting Instances

In classification problems, instances from underrepresented groups can be given higher weights during model training. This makes the model pay more attention to these instances and reduce bias.

b. Fair Representations

Fair representation learning aims to learn a feature space where the data distribution is as similar as possible across different groups. This can be achieved using techniques like adversarial networks or re-weighted loss functions.

3. Post-processing Techniques

a. Threshold Adjustments

By adjusting the decision thresholds of a model, we can control the trade-off between precision and recall, making the model's predictions fairer for different groups.

b. Reject Option Classification

Reject option classification allows a model to abstain from making predictions on instances it is uncertain about. This can help reduce bias in cases where the model is less confident.

4. Fairness Metrics

Evaluating model fairness is essential. Various fairness metrics, such as disparate impact, equal opportunity, and demographic parity, can be used to quantify bias in model predictions. Monitoring these metrics during model development and deployment is critical.

5. Continuous Monitoring

Bias in machine learning models can emerge or evolve over time. Therefore, continuous monitoring of model predictions, fairness metrics, and data sources is necessary. Organizations should establish mechanisms to detect and address bias as it arises.

6. Ethical Review Boards

Incorporating ethics into the development process requires input from diverse perspectives. Establishing ethical review boards or involving ethicists in the development process can help identify potential biases and ethical concerns.

7. Bias Audits

Conducting bias audits involves systematically examining the data, algorithms, and decision-making processes to identify and mitigate bias. Bias audits can be part of the model development lifecycle.

8. User Feedback

Feedback from users and stakeholders can provide valuable insights into potential biases or fairness issues in deployed machine learning systems. Organizations should create channels for users to report concerns.

9. Diversity in Development Teams

Diverse development teams that include individuals from various backgrounds and experiences are more likely to identify and address bias effectively. Encouraging diversity in AI development is essential.

In conclusion, mitigating bias in machine learning is a multidimensional and ongoing effort. It requires a combination of data preprocessing, algorithmic techniques, fairness metrics, monitoring, and ethical considerations. Addressing bias is not only an ethical imperative but also essential for building trust in machine learning systems and ensuring that AI benefits all members of society.

Section 15.4: Responsible AI Development

Developing machine learning models and AI systems responsibly is a critical aspect of ensuring that AI technologies have a positive impact on society. Responsible AI development encompasses a range of principles, practices, and guidelines that aim to address ethical, legal, and social considerations. In this section, we will explore key aspects of responsible AI development.

1. Data Privacy and Security

Data privacy is a fundamental concern in AI development. It involves ensuring that user data is handled in compliance with privacy regulations such as GDPR (General Data

Protection Regulation) or CCPA (California Consumer Privacy Act). Responsible AI developers must:

- **Anonymize Data:** Remove personally identifiable information (PII) from datasets used for training and testing.
- **Obtain Informed Consent:** Ensure that users are informed about how their data will be used and obtain their explicit consent.
- **Secure Data:** Implement robust data security measures to protect sensitive information from unauthorized access.

2. Transparency and Explainability

AI models should be transparent and explainable, allowing users to understand how decisions are made. Key practices include:

- **Model Explainability:** Use interpretable models or techniques that provide insights into the model's decision-making process.
- **Explainable AI Tools:** Employ tools and libraries that facilitate model interpretation, such as LIME (Local Interpretable Model-agnostic Explanations) or SHAP (SHapley Additive exPlanations).
- **Documentation:** Document model architectures, training processes, and decision logic comprehensively.

3. Fairness and Bias Mitigation

Responsible AI development includes strategies to mitigate bias and ensure fairness in AI systems. This involves:

- **Bias Assessment:** Conduct thorough bias assessments of AI models to identify and address disparities in model predictions.
- **Fairness-Aware Algorithms:** Explore fairness-aware machine learning algorithms that explicitly address fairness concerns.
- **Regular Audits:** Continuously monitor model performance and fairness metrics in real-world applications.

4. Accountability and Governance

Organizations should establish clear lines of accountability and governance for AI development. This includes:

- **Ethics Committees:** Form ethics committees or boards responsible for reviewing AI projects, assessing ethical considerations, and providing guidance.
- **Compliance:** Ensure that AI projects comply with legal and regulatory frameworks related to AI ethics and data protection.

5. User-Centric Design

User-centric design principles focus on creating AI systems that prioritize user well-being and satisfaction. Key considerations include:

- **Human-Centered AI:** Involve users and domain experts in the design process to understand their needs and concerns.
- **Feedback Loops:** Establish mechanisms for users to provide feedback and report issues with AI systems.

6. Accountability for Outcomes

Responsible AI development extends to accountability for outcomes. Developers and organizations should:

- **Accept Responsibility:** Take responsibility for the consequences of AI systems' actions and decisions.
- **Mitigate Harm:** Actively work to prevent and mitigate harm resulting from AI system errors or biases.
- **Redress Mechanisms:** Implement mechanisms to redress issues and provide remedies to affected parties.

7. Ethical Considerations

Ethical considerations should guide AI development. This includes:

- **Human Rights:** Ensure that AI systems respect fundamental human rights and do not infringe upon them.
- **Ethical Frameworks:** Adopt ethical frameworks and guidelines that align with societal values.

8. Public Engagement

Engaging with the public, stakeholders, and the broader community is essential for responsible AI development. This can involve:

- **Transparency Initiatives:** Share information about AI development practices and ethical commitments.
- **Public Input:** Seek input and feedback from the public and affected communities regarding AI deployments.

9. Continuous Learning and Improvement

Responsible AI development is an ongoing process. It requires:

- **Learning from Incidents:** Analyze and learn from incidents or cases where AI systems failed or caused harm.
- **Adaptation:** Adapt development practices based on emerging ethical considerations and best practices.

In conclusion, responsible AI development is crucial for creating AI systems that benefit society while minimizing risks and harm. It involves a holistic approach that considers data privacy, transparency, fairness, accountability, ethical considerations, and ongoing engagement with stakeholders. Embracing responsible AI practices is not only an ethical choice but also essential for building trust in AI technologies and ensuring their long-term success.

Section 15.5: Case Studies on Ethical Dilemmas

In this section, we will examine several case studies that highlight ethical dilemmas and challenges related to machine learning and artificial intelligence (AI) applications. These real-world examples underscore the importance of ethical considerations in AI development and the need for responsible practices.

Case Study 1: Predictive Policing Bias

Predictive policing systems use historical crime data to predict future crimes and allocate police resources. However, these systems have faced criticism for perpetuating bias in law enforcement. For example, if historical data reflects biased policing practices, predictive models may reinforce these biases.

Ethical Dilemma: Balancing the use of data-driven tools for crime prevention with concerns about exacerbating existing biases in policing.

Mitigation: Regularly audit predictive models for bias, employ fairness-aware algorithms, and involve communities in the design and oversight of these systems.

Case Study 2: Automated Hiring Algorithms

Some companies have adopted automated algorithms to assist in the hiring process. These algorithms analyze resumes and profiles to identify potential candidates. However, these systems have been criticized for inadvertently favoring certain demographics and perpetuating biases present in historical hiring data.

Ethical Dilemma: Addressing potential discrimination and fairness issues in automated hiring, particularly when algorithms may favor candidates from specific backgrounds.

Mitigation: Implement transparency in hiring algorithms, continuously audit for bias, and provide clear channels for candidates to appeal decisions.

Case Study 3: Autonomous Vehicles and Moral Dilemmas

Autonomous vehicles must make split-second decisions that can have ethical implications, such as deciding between saving the vehicle's occupants or avoiding harm to pedestrians. These moral dilemmas pose challenges in programming decision-making algorithms.

Ethical Dilemma: Defining the ethical framework for autonomous vehicles and determining how they should navigate moral dilemmas.

Mitigation: Establish clear ethical guidelines for autonomous vehicle behavior, prioritize safety, and involve ethicists and experts in AI ethics in decision-making.

Case Study 4: Deepfake Technology

Deepfake technology can create highly realistic, yet entirely fabricated, audio and video content. While it has legitimate applications, such as in filmmaking, it also poses significant risks for spreading misinformation, defamation, and fraud.

Ethical Dilemma: Balancing the creative and legitimate uses of deepfake technology with the potential for misuse and harm.

Mitigation: Develop methods to detect deepfake content, promote media literacy, and consider legal frameworks to address misuse.

Case Study 5: AI in Healthcare Diagnosis

Machine learning models are increasingly used in healthcare for disease diagnosis and treatment recommendations. However, concerns arise about the interpretability of AI models and the potential for misdiagnosis.

Ethical Dilemma: Ensuring the reliability and transparency of AI-driven healthcare solutions to prevent misdiagnosis and harm to patients.

Mitigation: Develop interpretable AI models, involve medical experts in model development, and implement strict validation and monitoring processes.

Case Study 6: Social Media Algorithms and Polarization

Social media platforms use recommendation algorithms to engage users. However, these algorithms have been criticized for contributing to echo chambers and political polarization by promoting content that aligns with users' existing views.

Ethical Dilemma: Balancing user engagement and platform profits with the societal impact of algorithmically driven content promotion.

Mitigation: Adjust recommendation algorithms to prioritize diverse content and consider regulatory measures to address the impact of algorithms on society.

These case studies illustrate that ethical dilemmas in AI and machine learning are complex and multifaceted. Addressing them requires a combination of technical, regulatory, and societal responses. Responsible AI development involves ongoing monitoring, adaptation, and collaboration among stakeholders to navigate these ethical challenges effectively.

Chapter 16: Real-World Machine Learning Projects

Section 16.1: Project Development Lifecycle

In this section, we will explore the project development lifecycle for real-world machine learning projects. Building and deploying machine learning solutions in a professional setting involves several stages, each with its unique challenges and considerations. Understanding this lifecycle is essential for successfully delivering ML projects.

The Machine Learning Project Lifecycle

1. Problem Definition and Planning

- **Define the Problem:** Clearly articulate the problem you aim to solve with machine learning.
- **Project Scope:** Determine the project's boundaries, objectives, and constraints.
- **Data Requirements:** Identify the data needed for training and evaluation.

2. Data Collection and Preparation

- **Data Gathering:** Acquire the necessary data from various sources.
- **Data Cleaning:** Clean the data by addressing missing values, outliers, and inconsistencies.
- **Feature Engineering:** Create relevant features from the raw data.
- **Data Splitting:** Divide the dataset into training, validation, and test sets.

3. Exploratory Data Analysis (EDA)

- **Data Exploration:** Analyze and visualize data to gain insights.
- **Statistical Analysis:** Perform statistical tests to understand relationships.
- **Feature Selection:** Identify essential features for model training.

4. Model Development

- **Model Selection:** Choose appropriate machine learning algorithms.
- **Model Training:** Train models using the training dataset.
- **Hyperparameter Tuning:** Optimize model hyperparameters for better performance.
- **Validation:** Evaluate models using the validation set to prevent overfitting.

5. Model Evaluation

- **Performance Metrics:** Select evaluation metrics (e.g., accuracy, F1-score) based on project goals.
- **Model Comparison:** Compare different models to choose the best one.
- **Ethical Considerations:** Assess the impact and potential biases of the model.

6. Model Deployment

- **Productionization:** Prepare the model for deployment in a production environment.
- **Scalability:** Ensure the model can handle real-world data volumes and requests.
- **Monitoring:** Implement monitoring and logging to track model performance.

7. Post-Deployment Maintenance

- **Continuous Improvement:** Update models with new data to maintain accuracy.
- **Bug Fixes:** Address issues and bugs as they arise in production.
- **Feedback Loop:** Gather feedback from end-users to inform improvements.

Collaboration and Documentation

Throughout the project lifecycle, collaboration among team members, including data scientists, engineers, domain experts, and stakeholders, is crucial. Effective documentation of the project's decisions, processes, and code ensures transparency and knowledge sharing.

Project Management Tools

Project management tools and methodologies, such as Agile or Scrum, can help streamline the development process, manage tasks, and maintain project timelines.

Ethical Considerations

Ethical considerations, especially in data collection and model deployment, should be central to the project development process. Mitigating bias, ensuring privacy, and addressing potential harm are critical aspects of responsible AI development.

By following this structured project development lifecycle, teams can increase the likelihood of delivering successful machine learning solutions that meet business objectives and ethical standards. Real-world ML projects often require adaptation and iteration as new insights emerge, making flexibility and continuous improvement key principles in AI development.

Section 16.2: Choosing the Right Project

Selecting the right machine learning project is a critical step in the development lifecycle. Choosing the wrong project can lead to wasted resources and effort. Here, we'll discuss the key factors to consider when selecting a machine learning project for real-world applications.

1. Business Impact

Start by evaluating the potential business impact of the project. Consider questions like: - Will the project solve a pressing business problem or enhance an existing process? - Can the project lead to cost savings, revenue generation, or improved customer satisfaction? - Does the project align with the organization's strategic goals and objectives?

A project with a clear and significant business impact is more likely to receive support and resources.

2. Data Availability

Ensure that the necessary data for the project is available or can be obtained. Consider: - Data Quality: Assess the quality and reliability of available data. - Data Accessibility: Confirm that you can access and use the data legally and ethically. - Data Volume: Evaluate whether the dataset is sufficient for model training.

Data availability is a critical factor that can determine the feasibility of a project.

3. Project Complexity

Assess the complexity of the project and its alignment with the team's capabilities. Consider factors like: - Technical Requirements: Does the project require specialized skills or tools? - Domain Knowledge: Do team members have expertise in the project's domain? - Project Duration: Is the project timeline feasible given its complexity?

Choosing a project that matches the team's skills and resources increases the chances of success.

4. Ethical and Regulatory Considerations

Consider the ethical and regulatory implications of the project. Evaluate: - Privacy: How will user data be handled, and are there privacy concerns? - Bias: Are there potential biases in the data or model that need mitigation? - Compliance: Ensure that the project complies with relevant laws and regulations (e.g., GDPR).

Addressing ethical and regulatory considerations is crucial for responsible AI development.

5. Project Resources

Determine the resources required for the project, including: - Data scientists and engineers - Hardware and software - Budget and funding - Stakeholder support

A clear understanding of resource needs is essential for project planning and execution.

6. Return on Investment (ROI)

Assess the expected return on investment for the project. Consider: - Cost-Benefit Analysis: Estimate the project's costs and potential benefits. - Risk Assessment: Identify potential risks and their impact on ROI. - Long-Term Viability: Evaluate whether the project can provide ongoing value.

Projects with a favorable ROI are more likely to be prioritized.

7. Alignment with User Needs

Consider the needs and preferences of end-users or customers. User-centric projects are more likely to succeed and provide value. Gather feedback from users to inform project decisions.

8. Scalability and Deployment

Think about how the project will be deployed at scale. Consider factors like: - Infrastructure requirements - Maintenance and updates - Integration with existing systems

A clear deployment plan ensures that the project can deliver value in the long term.

9. Alignment with Machine Learning Capabilities

Ensure that the project aligns with the capabilities of machine learning. Some problems are better suited for ML solutions than others. Consider: - Whether ML can provide a competitive advantage - The complexity of the problem space - Availability of relevant algorithms and models

Choosing a project that leverages the strengths of machine learning is essential.

10. Alignment with Organizational Culture

Consider the organization's culture and readiness for machine learning projects. Ensure that there is support and enthusiasm for AI initiatives among key stakeholders and team members.

In summary, selecting the right machine learning project involves a thorough evaluation of business impact, data availability, project complexity, ethical considerations, resources, ROI, user needs, scalability, alignment with ML capabilities, and organizational culture. By carefully assessing these factors, you can increase the likelihood of a successful and impactful machine learning project.

Section 16.3: Data Collection and Annotation

Data collection and annotation are foundational steps in the development of a machine learning project. In this section, we'll explore the importance of data collection, methods for gathering data, and the process of annotating data for supervised learning.

The Importance of Data Collection

Data is the lifeblood of machine learning. The quality and quantity of data you collect directly impact the performance of your machine learning models. Here are some key considerations regarding data collection:

1. **Representativeness**: Ensure that your data is representative of the problem you're trying to solve. Biased or unrepresentative data can lead to biased models.

2. **Volume**: More data is often better, but it's important to strike a balance. Collecting too much data can be costly and time-consuming.

3. **Quality**: High-quality data is essential. This includes accurate labels, minimal noise, and complete information.

4. **Ethical Considerations**: Respect user privacy and obtain data legally and ethically. Follow relevant regulations, such as GDPR.

Methods of Data Collection

There are several methods for collecting data, depending on the nature of your project:

1. **Web Scraping**: Gather data from websites and online sources using web scraping tools and techniques. Be mindful of website terms of service and copyright issues.

2. **Surveys and Questionnaires**: Create surveys to collect structured data from users. Surveys can be useful for gathering feedback or preferences.

3. **Sensor Data**: In IoT and sensor-based applications, data can be collected from physical sensors, such as temperature sensors, cameras, or GPS devices.

4. **APIs**: Access data through APIs (Application Programming Interfaces) provided by online platforms and services. This method is common for social media data or financial data.

5. **Manual Entry**: Sometimes, data needs to be entered manually. This can be labor-intensive and error-prone, so careful validation is essential.

6. **Existing Datasets**: Many public datasets are available for various domains. You can use these datasets as a starting point for your project.

Data Annotation

In supervised learning, data annotation involves labeling data points with the correct target values. For example, in an image classification project, annotators might label images with corresponding categories.

Key considerations for data annotation:

1. **Annotation Guidelines**: Provide clear guidelines to annotators to ensure consistent labeling. Training annotators may be necessary.

2. **Quality Control**: Implement quality control measures to identify and correct annotation errors. This may involve double-checking or using multiple annotators.

3. **Iterative Process**: Data annotation can be an iterative process. As you train initial models, you may discover the need for additional annotations or corrections.

4. **Scalability**: Consider how to scale data annotation as your dataset grows. Crowdsourcing platforms or specialized annotation tools can be helpful.

5. **Time and Cost**: Data annotation can be time-consuming and costly. Plan your budget and timeline accordingly.

6. **Privacy and Confidentiality**: Ensure that sensitive data is handled with care and in compliance with privacy regulations.

Tools and Platforms

There are various tools and platforms available to assist with data collection and annotation. These include:

- Labeling tools for annotating images, videos, and text.
- Crowdsourcing platforms like Amazon Mechanical Turk for large-scale annotation tasks.
- Data management systems for organizing and storing collected data.

In conclusion, data collection and annotation are crucial steps in preparing data for machine learning. The quality, quantity, and ethical handling of data are essential considerations. By following best practices and leveraging appropriate tools, you can build a robust dataset to train your machine learning models effectively.

Section 16.4: Building and Iterating Models

Once you have collected and annotated your data, the next step in a machine learning project is to build and iterate on your models. This section will guide you through the process of model development and refinement.

Model Development

Data Splitting

Before you can train and evaluate a machine learning model, it's essential to split your dataset into three parts: training, validation, and test sets. The training set is used to train the model, the validation set helps in tuning hyperparameters, and the test set assesses the model's performance.

```
from sklearn.model_selection import train_test_split

# Split data into training, validation, and test sets
X_train, X_temp, y_train, y_temp = train_test_split(X, y, test_size=0.3, rand
om_state=42)
X_val, X_test, y_val, y_test = train_test_split(X_temp, y_temp, test_size=0.5
, random_state=42)
```

Model Training

Select an appropriate machine learning algorithm for your task and train the model using the training data. The choice of algorithm depends on whether you're working on a classification or regression problem, among other factors.

```python
from sklearn.tree import DecisionTreeClassifier

# Initialize and train a decision tree classifier
clf = DecisionTreeClassifier()
clf.fit(X_train, y_train)
```

Hyperparameter Tuning

Fine-tune the model's hyperparameters using the validation set. Techniques like grid search or random search can help find the best hyperparameters for your model.

```python
from sklearn.model_selection import GridSearchCV

# Define hyperparameter grid for grid search
param_grid = {'max_depth': [2, 4, 6, 8], 'min_samples_split': [2, 5, 10]}

# Initialize grid search with cross-validation
grid_search = GridSearchCV(clf, param_grid, cv=5)
grid_search.fit(X_train, y_train)

# Get the best hyperparameters
best_params = grid_search.best_params_
```

Model Evaluation and Refinement

Evaluation Metrics

Evaluate your model's performance on the validation set using appropriate evaluation metrics such as accuracy, precision, recall, F1-score, or mean squared error, depending on the problem type.

```python
from sklearn.metrics import accuracy_score

# Make predictions on the validation set
y_val_pred = grid_search.predict(X_val)

# Calculate accuracy
accuracy = accuracy_score(y_val, y_val_pred)
```

Model Iteration

Based on the validation results, you may need to iterate on your model. This could involve adjusting hyperparameters, trying different algorithms, or engineering new features.

```
# Example of hyperparameter adjustment based on validation results
clf = DecisionTreeClassifier(max_depth=best_params['max_depth'], min_samples_
split=best_params['min_samples_split'])
clf.fit(X_train, y_train)
```

Overfitting and Underfitting

Watch out for overfitting (high training performance but poor validation performance) and underfitting (poor training and validation performance). Adjust model complexity and regularization to mitigate these issues.

Conclusion

Building and iterating on machine learning models is an iterative process that involves data splitting, model training, hyperparameter tuning, and evaluation. Regularly assess your model's performance and refine it as needed to achieve the desired results on the validation set. In the next section, we will explore the deployment and maintenance of machine learning models in a real-world context.

Section 16.5: Deployment and Maintenance

In the final stages of a machine learning project, after you have developed and fine-tuned your model, it's time to deploy it into a production environment. This section covers the deployment and maintenance aspects of machine learning models.

Deployment Considerations

Model Export

Before deploying your model, you need to export it into a format that can be used for predictions. Most machine learning libraries provide functions or tools to save your trained model to a file.

```
import joblib

# Save the trained model to a file
joblib.dump(clf, 'model.pkl')
```

Building APIs

To make predictions using your model, you can build a RESTful API using web frameworks like Flask or FastAPI. This allows other applications to send data to your model and receive predictions in real-time.

```
from flask import Flask, request, jsonify

app = Flask(__name__)
```

```python
@app.route('/predict', methods=['POST'])
def predict():
    # Receive input data
    data = request.json

    # Perform prediction using the model
    prediction = clf.predict(data)

    # Return the prediction as JSON
    return jsonify({'prediction': prediction.tolist()})

if __name__ == '__main__':
    app.run(debug=True)
```

Containerization with Docker

Containerization with Docker allows you to package your model and its dependencies into a standardized container that can run consistently across different environments.

Dockerfile

Create a Dockerfile that specifies the environment and dependencies needed to run your model.

```dockerfile
# Use an official Python runtime as a parent image
FROM python:3.7-slim

# Set the working directory to /app
WORKDIR /app

# Copy the current directory contents into the container at /app
COPY . /app

# Install any needed packages specified in requirements.txt
RUN pip install -r requirements.txt

# Make port 80 available to the world outside this container
EXPOSE 80

# Define environment variable
ENV NAME World

# Run app.py when the container launches
CMD ["python", "app.py"]
```

Building and Running the Docker Container

Build the Docker container using the docker build command and run it with docker run.

```
docker build -t my-model .
docker run -p 4000:80 my-model
```

Cloud Deployment

You can deploy your machine learning model on cloud platforms like AWS, Azure, or Google Cloud Platform (GCP). These platforms provide scalable and managed environments for running machine learning workloads.

AWS Lambda

AWS Lambda is a serverless compute service that allows you to run code without provisioning or managing servers. You can deploy your model as a Lambda function and expose it as an API using Amazon API Gateway.

Azure Functions

Azure Functions is a serverless compute service on Azure. You can create an Azure Function to serve your model predictions and integrate it with Azure API Management for API hosting.

Google Cloud Functions

Google Cloud Functions is Google's serverless compute service. You can deploy your model as a function and use Google Cloud Endpoints to manage and expose your API.

Monitoring and Scaling

Once your model is deployed, it's essential to monitor its performance and scale it according to demand. Implement logging and monitoring to track predictions, errors, and resource utilization.

Logging

Use logging libraries to record events and errors in your deployed model. This helps in diagnosing issues and improving model performance.

```python
import logging

logging.basicConfig(level=logging.INFO)
logger = logging.getLogger(__name__)

def predict():
    try:
        # Perform prediction using the model
        prediction = clf.predict(data)
        logger.info(f"Prediction: {prediction}")
        return jsonify({'prediction': prediction.tolist()})
    except Exception as e:
        logger.error(f"Prediction failed: {str(e)}")
        return jsonify({'error': 'Prediction failed'}), 500
```

Scaling

Configure your deployment to scale automatically based on demand. Use auto-scaling features provided by cloud platforms or container orchestration tools like Kubernetes.

Conclusion

Deployment and maintenance are crucial steps in turning a machine learning model into a real-world solution. Whether you choose to deploy locally with Flask, containerize with Docker, or use cloud platforms, it's essential to ensure your model performs well in a production environment and can handle the expected workload. Regularly monitor and maintain your deployed model to keep it accurate and reliable over time. This concludes our journey through the machine learning lifecycle.

Chapter 17: Case Studies in Industry

Section 17.1: Machine Learning in Healthcare

Machine learning has made significant strides in the healthcare industry, revolutionizing how medical data is analyzed, diagnoses are made, and patient care is delivered. In this section, we'll explore the various applications of machine learning in healthcare.

Electronic Health Records (EHR)

One of the fundamental applications of machine learning in healthcare is the analysis of electronic health records (EHRs). Machine learning models can help healthcare providers sift through vast amounts of patient data, identify trends, and predict health outcomes. For example, ML models can assist in identifying patients at risk of specific diseases based on their medical history and lab results.

```python
# Example of using machine learning for risk prediction
from sklearn.model_selection import train_test_split
from sklearn.ensemble import RandomForestClassifier

# Load and preprocess EHR data
X, y = load_ehr_data()
X_train, X_test, y_train, y_test = train_test_split(X, y, test_size=0.2, rand
om_state=42)

# Train a Random Forest classifier
clf = RandomForestClassifier()
clf.fit(X_train, y_train)

# Make predictions on new patient data
predictions = clf.predict(X_test)
```

Medical Imaging

Machine learning has brought transformative changes to medical imaging, enabling more accurate and faster diagnoses. Deep learning models, especially convolutional neural networks (CNNs), have demonstrated exceptional performance in tasks such as image classification, object detection, and segmentation. For instance, CNNs can assist radiologists in detecting abnormalities in X-rays, MRIs, and CT scans.

```python
# Example of using a CNN for medical image classification
from tensorflow import keras
from tensorflow.keras import layers

# Build a CNN model for image classification
model = keras.Sequential([
    layers.Conv2D(32, (3, 3), activation='relu', input_shape=(128, 128, 3)),
```

```python
    layers.MaxPooling2D((2, 2)),
    layers.Flatten(),
    layers.Dense(64, activation='relu'),
    layers.Dense(10, activation='softmax')
])

# Compile and train the model using medical image data
model.compile(optimizer='adam',
              loss='sparse_categorical_crossentropy',
              metrics=['accuracy'])
model.fit(train_images, train_labels, epochs=10)
```

Drug Discovery and Genomics

Machine learning plays a crucial role in drug discovery and genomics research. ML models are used to analyze genomic data, identify potential drug candidates, and predict how drugs will interact with specific genetic profiles. This accelerates the drug development process and allows for personalized medicine approaches.

```python
# Example of using machine learning in drug discovery
from sklearn.ensemble import RandomForestRegressor

# Load genomics and drug response data
X_genomics, y_drug_response = load_genomics_and_drug_data()

# Train a regression model to predict drug response
regressor = RandomForestRegressor()
regressor.fit(X_genomics, y_drug_response)

# Predict drug response for new compounds
predicted_response = regressor.predict(new_compound_genomics)
```

Telemedicine and Remote Monitoring

Telemedicine and remote monitoring have become increasingly important, especially in remote or underserved areas. Machine learning is used to develop remote patient monitoring systems that can detect anomalies and alert healthcare providers in real-time. This allows for early intervention and improved patient care.

```python
# Example of using ML for remote patient monitoring
from sklearn.ensemble import IsolationForest

# Collect vital signs data from remote patients
vital_signs = collect_vital_signs()

# Detect anomalies in vital signs data
anomaly_detector = IsolationForest()
anomalies = anomaly_detector.fit_predict(vital_signs)

# Alert healthcare providers for further evaluation if anomalies are detected
```

```python
if any(anomalies == -1):
    send_alert("Anomalies detected in patient vital signs.")
```

Ethical Considerations

While the applications of machine learning in healthcare are promising, they also raise ethical and privacy concerns. Ensuring the security and privacy of patient data, as well as addressing biases in algorithms, is of utmost importance. Additionally, regulatory compliance, such as HIPAA in the United States, must be adhered to when handling healthcare data.

In conclusion, machine learning has the potential to revolutionize healthcare by improving diagnosis accuracy, drug discovery, and remote patient monitoring. However, it must be implemented responsibly, with a focus on patient privacy and ethical considerations.

Section 17.2: Financial Services and Risk Assessment

Machine learning has found extensive applications in the financial services industry, particularly in risk assessment, fraud detection, and algorithmic trading. In this section, we'll delve into the various ways in which machine learning is transforming the world of finance.

Credit Risk Assessment

One of the most prominent applications of machine learning in finance is credit risk assessment. Traditional credit scoring models are often based on a limited set of features and may not capture the full financial profile of an individual or business. Machine learning models, on the other hand, can leverage a wide range of data sources to assess creditworthiness more accurately.

```python
# Example of using machine learning for credit risk assessment
from sklearn.model_selection import train_test_split
from sklearn.ensemble import RandomForestClassifier

# Load and preprocess credit data
X, y = load_credit_data()
X_train, X_test, y_train, y_test = train_test_split(X, y, test_size=0.2, rand
om_state=42)

# Train a Random Forest classifier
clf = RandomForestClassifier()
clf.fit(X_train, y_train)

# Make credit approval predictions
predictions = clf.predict(X_test)
```

Fraud Detection

Machine learning is indispensable in the fight against financial fraud. ML models can analyze transaction data in real-time to detect unusual patterns or anomalies that may indicate fraudulent activity. This proactive approach helps financial institutions prevent losses and protect their customers.

```python
# Example of using machine learning for fraud detection
from sklearn.ensemble import IsolationForest

# Collect transaction data
transactions = collect_transactions()

# Detect anomalies in transaction data
anomaly_detector = IsolationForest()
anomalies = anomaly_detector.fit_predict(transactions)

# Flag and investigate potentially fraudulent transactions
fraudulent_transactions = transactions[anomalies == -1]
```

Algorithmic Trading

Algorithmic trading, also known as quantitative trading or algo trading, relies heavily on machine learning to make rapid and data-driven trading decisions. ML models can analyze historical price data, news sentiment, and other factors to execute trades with high accuracy and speed.

```python
# Example of using machine learning in algorithmic trading
import pandas as pd
from sklearn.ensemble import RandomForestClassifier

# Load and preprocess historical price and sentiment data
data = load_trading_data()
X, y = preprocess_data(data)

# Train a trading model
clf = RandomForestClassifier()
clf.fit(X, y)

# Make real-time trading decisions based on model predictions
current_data = fetch_current_data()
trade_signal = clf.predict(current_data)
```

Regulatory Compliance

Machine learning also plays a crucial role in ensuring regulatory compliance in the financial sector. ML models can monitor transactions for suspicious activities and generate reports to meet regulatory requirements, such as Anti-Money Laundering (AML) and Know Your Customer (KYC) regulations.

```
# Example of using ML for regulatory compliance
from sklearn.ensemble import IsolationForest

# Collect transaction data for AML monitoring
transactions = collect_transactions()

# Detect anomalies in transaction data
anomaly_detector = IsolationForest()
anomalies = anomaly_detector.fit_predict(transactions)

# Generate reports on potentially suspicious transactions for AML compliance
suspicious_transactions = transactions[anomalies == -1]
generate_aml_report(suspicious_transactions)
```

Ethical Considerations

While machine learning offers numerous advantages in the financial services industry, it also poses ethical challenges. Fair lending practices, transparency in algorithmic decision-making, and protecting customer data privacy are critical considerations. Financial institutions must strike a balance between innovation and responsibility when implementing machine learning solutions.

In summary, machine learning is transforming the financial services sector by improving credit risk assessment, enhancing fraud detection, enabling algorithmic trading, and ensuring regulatory compliance. However, ethical considerations and responsible use of AI are paramount in maintaining trust and integrity in the industry.

Section 17.3: E-commerce and Recommendation Systems

E-commerce has experienced significant growth over the past decade, driven by technological advancements and changing consumer behavior. Machine learning plays a pivotal role in this sector, particularly in the domain of recommendation systems. In this section, we'll explore how recommendation systems powered by ML are reshaping the e-commerce landscape.

Personalized Product Recommendations

One of the key features that enhance the user experience in e-commerce platforms is personalized product recommendations. Machine learning algorithms analyze user behavior, purchase history, and preferences to suggest products that are highly relevant to individual users. These recommendations can significantly boost sales and customer engagement.

```
# Example of user-based collaborative filtering for product recommendations
import pandas as pd
from sklearn.metrics.pairwise import cosine_similarity
```

```
# Load user interaction data
user_data = load_user_data()

# Compute user similarity based on their interactions
user_similarity = cosine_similarity(user_data)

# Recommend products for a specific user
user_id = 123
user_interactions = user_data[user_id]
similar_users = user_similarity[user_id]

# Sort products by similarity and recommend the top ones
recommended_products = sort_products_by_similarity(user_interactions, similar
_users)
```

Content-Based Recommendations

Content-based recommendation systems leverage the attributes of products and user profiles to make recommendations. Machine learning models analyze product descriptions, attributes, and user preferences to suggest items that align with a user's interests.

```
# Example of content-based recommendation using TF-IDF and cosine similarity
from sklearn.feature_extraction.text import TfidfVectorizer

# Load product data and user preferences
product_data = load_product_data()
user_preferences = load_user_preferences()

# Create TF-IDF vectors for product descriptions
tfidf_vectorizer = TfidfVectorizer()
product_descriptions = product_data['description']
tfidf_matrix = tfidf_vectorizer.fit_transform(product_descriptions)

# Calculate cosine similarity between user preferences and product descriptio
ns
user_id = 123
user_preference_vector = user_preferences[user_id]
cosine_similarities = cosine_similarity(user_preference_vector, tfidf_matrix)

# Recommend products based on similarity scores
recommended_products = recommend_products_by_similarity(cosine_similarities)
```

Real-Time Recommendations

Machine learning models can also provide real-time recommendations to users as they browse an e-commerce website or app. These recommendations take into account the user's current session, search queries, and interactions to suggest products that are immediately relevant.

```
# Example of real-time recommendation using session data
from sklearn.ensemble import RandomForestClassifier

# Load and preprocess session data
session_data = load_session_data()
X, y = preprocess_session_data(session_data)

# Train a recommendation model
clf = RandomForestClassifier()
clf.fit(X, y)

# Provide real-time recommendations during a user's session
current_session_data = fetch_current_session_data()
recommended_products = clf.predict(current_session_data)
```

Upselling and Cross-Selling

Recommendation systems are also instrumental in upselling and cross-selling strategies. By analyzing a user's purchase history and behavior, machine learning models can suggest complementary products or premium versions of items that align with the user's preferences.

Ethical Considerations

While recommendation systems offer tremendous benefits in e-commerce, there are ethical considerations regarding user privacy and data usage. It's essential for e-commerce platforms to be transparent about their recommendation algorithms, obtain user consent for data collection, and ensure data security to maintain trust with their customers.

In summary, machine learning-driven recommendation systems are pivotal in e-commerce, providing personalized product recommendations, enhancing user engagement, and driving sales. However, e-commerce companies must prioritize ethical considerations to protect user privacy and maintain customer trust.

Section 17.4: Autonomous Vehicles and Robotics

The application of machine learning in autonomous vehicles and robotics has revolutionized transportation and automation industries. In this section, we'll explore how machine learning technologies have enabled the development of self-driving cars and advanced robotics systems.

Self-Driving Cars

Self-driving cars, also known as autonomous vehicles, are equipped with sensors, cameras, and machine learning algorithms that allow them to navigate roads without human intervention. These vehicles use a combination of computer vision, sensor fusion, and deep learning to perceive their surroundings and make real-time decisions.

Computer vision plays a crucial role in self-driving cars. Machine learning models are trained to detect objects such as pedestrians, other vehicles, traffic signs, and obstacles. Convolutional Neural Networks (CNNs) are commonly used for object detection tasks.

```python
# Example of object detection using a pre-trained CNN model
import cv2
import numpy as np

# Load a pre-trained CNN model
model = load_pretrained_cnn_model()

# Capture video feed from the car's cameras
video_capture = cv2.VideoCapture('camera_feed.mp4')

while True:
    # Read a frame from the camera
    ret, frame = video_capture.read()

    # Perform object detection using the CNN model
    detected_objects = detect_objects(frame, model)

    # Make driving decisions based on detected objects
    make_driving_decision(detected_objects)
```

Sensor Fusion for Localization

Self-driving cars use a combination of sensors, including LiDAR, radar, and GPS, to accurately localize themselves within their environment. Machine learning algorithms fuse data from these sensors to create a precise representation of the car's position and surroundings.

Robotics and Automation

Machine learning has also transformed the field of robotics. Robots are now capable of performing complex tasks, such as object manipulation, path planning, and even learning from human demonstrations.

Reinforcement Learning for Robot Control

Reinforcement learning is used to train robots to perform tasks through trial and error. Robots receive rewards or penalties based on their actions, allowing them to learn optimal strategies for tasks like picking and placing objects.

```python
# Example of reinforcement learning for robot control
import gym
import reinforcement_learning_algorithm as rl

# Define the robot control environment
```

```
env = gym.make('robot-control-v0')

# Create a reinforcement learning agent
agent = rl.Agent()

# Train the agent to perform a specific task
agent.train(env)
```

Collaborative Robots (Cobots)

Collaborative robots, or cobots, work alongside humans in industrial settings. These robots use machine learning to adapt to human behavior and perform tasks collaboratively. Safety is a paramount consideration in cobot design, and machine learning algorithms are used to detect and avoid collisions with humans.

Ethical Considerations

The deployment of self-driving cars and advanced robotics raises ethical questions related to safety, liability, and job displacement. Ensuring the safety of autonomous systems, establishing clear regulations, and addressing societal concerns are critical aspects of integrating machine learning into these domains.

In conclusion, machine learning has paved the way for self-driving cars and advanced robotics, offering the potential to transform transportation and automation industries. However, ethical considerations and safety precautions must be at the forefront of these developments to ensure their responsible and beneficial integration into society.

Section 17.5: Impact of ML on Various Industries

Machine learning (ML) has had a profound impact on various industries, revolutionizing the way businesses operate and make decisions. In this section, we will explore how ML has transformed different sectors and discuss some notable examples.

Healthcare

ML has made significant contributions to healthcare, improving diagnostics, treatment plans, and patient care. Machine learning models can analyze medical images, such as X-rays and MRIs, to detect diseases and abnormalities with high accuracy. Natural language processing (NLP) is used for analyzing clinical notes and research papers, aiding in research and decision-making.

Example: Disease Detection

Machine learning algorithms can predict the likelihood of diseases such as diabetes, cancer, and heart disease. For instance, predictive models analyze patient data to identify individuals at risk, enabling early intervention and personalized treatment plans.

Financial Services

The financial industry relies heavily on ML for risk assessment, fraud detection, and algorithmic trading. ML models analyze vast datasets to identify patterns and anomalies, helping financial institutions make informed decisions and minimize risks.

Example: Credit Scoring

Banks and lending institutions use ML-based credit scoring models to assess the creditworthiness of applicants. These models consider various factors, including credit history, income, and spending habits, to determine the likelihood of repayment.

E-commerce

E-commerce platforms leverage ML for recommendation systems, personalization, and fraud prevention. ML algorithms analyze user behavior and product data to suggest relevant products, increasing user engagement and sales.

Example: Product Recommendations

Online retailers like Amazon and Netflix use ML algorithms to recommend products and content based on a user's past interactions and preferences. This enhances the user experience and drives sales.

Manufacturing

ML plays a crucial role in optimizing manufacturing processes and predictive maintenance. Sensors and IoT devices collect real-time data, which ML models analyze to identify equipment failures and schedule maintenance proactively.

Example: Predictive Maintenance

In manufacturing plants, ML algorithms predict when machinery is likely to fail, allowing for scheduled maintenance and preventing costly downtime.

Transportation and Logistics

ML is used in transportation and logistics to optimize routes, manage fleets, and enhance safety. Self-driving trucks and drones rely on ML for autonomous navigation.

Example: Route Optimization

Delivery companies use ML to find the most efficient delivery routes, considering factors like traffic, weather, and package weight.

Entertainment and Media

ML is employed in the entertainment industry for content recommendation, video analysis, and personalization. Streaming platforms use ML to suggest movies and shows based on viewers' preferences.

Example: Content Recommendation

Example: Content Recommendation

Video streaming services like YouTube and Netflix use ML algorithms to recommend content tailored to individual users, increasing viewer engagement.

Agriculture

ML is transforming agriculture by enabling precision farming. Drones equipped with ML-powered cameras monitor crop health, and predictive models help optimize planting and harvesting schedules.

Example: Crop Yield Prediction

Farmers use ML to predict crop yields based on weather conditions, soil quality, and historical data. This allows for better resource allocation and planning.

These examples highlight the diverse applications of ML across various industries. As technology continues to advance, the integration of ML into these sectors will likely expand, driving innovation and efficiency. However, it is essential to address challenges such as data privacy, bias, and ethical considerations to ensure that ML benefits society as a whole.

Chapter 18: Future Trends in Machine Learning

Section 18.1: Current Trends and Challenges

Machine learning (ML) is a dynamic field, constantly evolving with new trends, technologies, and challenges. In this section, we'll explore some of the current trends shaping the future of ML and the associated challenges.

1. Explainable AI (XAI)

One significant trend is the growing emphasis on Explainable AI (XAI). As ML models become more complex, there is a need for transparency and interpretability. XAI aims to make ML models more understandable by providing insights into their decision-making processes. This is crucial in applications like healthcare and finance, where model decisions can have significant consequences.

2. Quantum Machine Learning

Quantum computing holds the promise of solving complex problems much faster than classical computers. In ML, quantum computing can potentially revolutionize optimization tasks, leading to breakthroughs in areas like drug discovery, cryptography, and more.

3. Federated Learning

Federated learning allows ML models to be trained across decentralized edge devices while keeping data localized. This enhances privacy and security, making it suitable for applications in healthcare, finance, and IoT. However, federated learning introduces challenges related to model aggregation and communication efficiency.

4. Ethical AI and Regulation

As ML is integrated into critical systems, the need for ethical considerations and regulations becomes paramount. Ensuring fairness, transparency, and accountability in ML systems is an ongoing challenge. Governments and organizations worldwide are developing regulations and guidelines to address these concerns.

5. AutoML and Democratization

AutoML tools and platforms are making ML more accessible to non-experts. This democratization of ML enables individuals and small businesses to leverage ML for various applications without extensive technical expertise. However, it also raises concerns about the responsible use of these tools.

6. Natural Language Processing Advancements

Advancements in natural language processing (NLP) are leading to more sophisticated conversational AI, language translation, and sentiment analysis. These developments have applications in customer support, content generation, and cross-language communication.

7. Reinforcement Learning in Robotics

Reinforcement learning (RL) is gaining traction in robotics, enabling machines to learn through trial and error. RL-powered robots are used in scenarios like autonomous vehicles, warehouse automation, and healthcare assistance.

While these trends hold immense potential, they also come with challenges. ML practitioners must address issues of bias and fairness, data privacy, model robustness, and ethical considerations. Moreover, keeping up with the rapid pace of innovation in the field requires continuous learning and adaptation.

In this ever-evolving landscape, staying informed about the latest developments, participating in the ML community, and embracing ethical practices are essential for harnessing the full potential of machine learning while ensuring its responsible and equitable use. The future of ML is exciting, but it also demands vigilance and responsibility from all stakeholders.

Section 18.2: Explainable AI (XAI)

Explainable AI (XAI) is a crucial aspect of machine learning and artificial intelligence. As machine learning models, particularly deep neural networks, become increasingly complex, it becomes challenging to understand how these models make decisions. XAI aims to address this issue by making machine learning models more transparent and interpretable.

In this section, we will delve into the concept of XAI, its importance, and some techniques used to achieve it.

Importance of Explainable AI

1. Trust and Accountability

One of the primary reasons for the growing interest in XAI is trust and accountability. In critical applications like healthcare, finance, and autonomous vehicles, users and stakeholders need to trust the decisions made by AI systems. When these decisions are explainable, users can better understand and trust the technology.

2. Legal and Ethical Compliance

Legal and ethical considerations are becoming increasingly important in AI applications. Regulations like the General Data Protection Regulation (GDPR) in Europe require organizations to provide explanations for automated decisions that affect individuals. XAI helps organizations comply with such regulations.

3. Debugging and Improvement

Explainable AI aids in model debugging and improvement. When a model's behavior is explainable, data scientists and machine learning engineers can diagnose issues and fine-tune models more effectively. This leads to better performance and reliability.

XAI Techniques

Several techniques are employed to make AI models explainable:

1. Feature Importance

Feature importance techniques, such as permutation importance and SHAP (SHapley Additive exPlanations), help determine the contribution of each input feature to a model's prediction. This information can be visualized to show which features have the most significant impact on the output.

2. Local Explanations

Local explanation methods, like LIME (Local Interpretable Model-Agnostic Explanations), focus on explaining individual predictions. They create simplified, interpretable models that approximate the behavior of the complex model for a specific instance.

3. Saliency Maps

In computer vision, saliency maps highlight the regions of an image that contribute most to a model's prediction. Techniques like Grad-CAM (Gradient-weighted Class Activation Mapping) generate these maps, making it clear which parts of an image the model is paying attention to.

Rule-based models, such as decision trees and rule lists, are inherently interpretable. They can be used to approximate the behavior of more complex models, providing transparent decision-making.

5. Model-Agnostic Methods

Model-agnostic methods, like SHAP and LIME mentioned earlier, are not tied to a specific machine learning algorithm. They can be applied to any model, making them versatile tools for XAI.

Challenges and Trade-Offs

While XAI is essential, it comes with challenges and trade-offs. Simplifying models for interpretability may lead to a loss of predictive performance. Additionally, some complex models, like deep neural networks, are inherently challenging to explain comprehensively.

In conclusion, Explainable AI is a critical component of responsible AI development. It enhances trust, ensures legal compliance, aids in model improvement, and helps with debugging. XAI techniques, such as feature importance, local explanations, saliency maps, rule-based models, and model-agnostic methods, provide various options for making AI models more transparent. However, practitioners must carefully balance the need for explainability with model performance, recognizing that there may be trade-offs between the two.

Section 18.3: Quantum Machine Learning

Quantum Machine Learning (QML) represents a promising intersection of quantum computing and machine learning. Quantum computers, which leverage the principles of quantum mechanics, offer the potential to solve certain computational problems significantly faster than classical computers. This section explores the concept of Quantum Machine Learning, its applications, and its implications for the future of the field.

Key Concepts in Quantum Computing

Before diving into Quantum Machine Learning, let's briefly review some fundamental concepts in quantum computing:

1. Qubits

In classical computing, we use bits as the fundamental unit of information, which can represent either 0 or 1. In quantum computing, we use qubits, which can exist in multiple states simultaneously, thanks to the principle of superposition. This property allows quantum computers to process a vast amount of information in parallel.

2. Entanglement

Entanglement is another essential property of qubits. When qubits are entangled, the state of one qubit becomes dependent on the state of another, even when separated by large distances. This property is at the heart of many quantum algorithms.

3. Quantum Gates

Quantum gates are the equivalent of classical logic gates in quantum computing. They manipulate qubits to perform various operations. Notable quantum gates include the Hadamard gate and the CNOT gate.

Applications of Quantum Machine Learning

Quantum Machine Learning holds significant promise in various domains:

1. Speeding Up Optimization Problems

Quantum computers have demonstrated the potential to solve complex optimization problems much faster than classical computers. This capability is particularly valuable in logistics, supply chain management, and financial modeling.

2. Enhancing Machine Learning Algorithms

Quantum algorithms can improve machine learning tasks like clustering, classification, and dimensionality reduction. Quantum versions of classical algorithms may outperform their classical counterparts in specific scenarios.

3. Quantum Neural Networks

Quantum Neural Networks (QNNs) use quantum circuits to perform machine learning tasks. They have the potential to handle large datasets more efficiently and may uncover patterns that classical neural networks struggle to detect.

Challenges and Limitations

Despite its promise, Quantum Machine Learning faces several challenges:

1. Hardware Limitations

Quantum computers are still in the early stages of development, and building practical, error-corrected quantum hardware remains a formidable challenge.

2. Algorithm Development

Developing quantum algorithms for machine learning tasks requires expertise in both quantum computing and machine learning, limiting the number of researchers who can contribute to this field.

Identifying scenarios where quantum computers outperform classical computers remains an ongoing research question. Not all problems will benefit from quantum acceleration.

Future Directions

The future of Quantum Machine Learning is closely tied to advancements in quantum hardware, algorithm development, and real-world applications. As quantum computing technology matures, we can expect to see more practical applications of QML in fields such as cryptography, drug discovery, and artificial intelligence.

In conclusion, Quantum Machine Learning represents an exciting frontier in both quantum computing and machine learning. While it is still in its early stages, the potential to solve complex problems more efficiently and unlock new capabilities is driving significant research and innovation in this field. As quantum hardware continues to evolve, we can anticipate groundbreaking applications that leverage the power of quantum computing for machine learning tasks.

Section 18.4: Federated Learning

Federated Learning is an emerging machine learning paradigm designed to address privacy and data decentralization challenges. It allows multiple parties or devices to collaboratively train a machine learning model without sharing their raw data. In this section, we'll delve into the concept of Federated Learning, its applications, and its significance in the future of machine learning.

How Federated Learning Works

Federated Learning operates on the principle of decentralized model training. Here's a high-level overview of the process:

1. **Initialization**: A global model is created and initialized on a central server.

2. **Local Training**: Each participating device or party, often referred to as a "client," downloads the global model. These clients perform local training on their respective datasets, using techniques like stochastic gradient descent (SGD).

3. **Model Updates**: After local training, clients compute model updates based on their datasets and send only these updates, not their raw data, back to the central server.

4. **Aggregation**: The central server aggregates the received model updates to create an improved global model. This process typically involves techniques like weighted averaging.

5. **Iterative Process**: Steps 2 to 4 are repeated iteratively, allowing the global model to improve without exposing sensitive data.

Privacy and Security Benefits

Federated Learning offers several advantages, primarily centered around privacy and security:

1. Data Privacy

Since raw data remains on clients and is not shared with a central server, Federated Learning helps protect user privacy. This is especially important for applications like healthcare and finance, where data sensitivity is paramount.

2. Data Efficiency

Federated Learning enables model training on decentralized data sources, reducing the need for large-scale data centralization. This can save bandwidth and storage costs.

3. Security

By keeping data local, Federated Learning reduces the risk of data breaches or unauthorized access. Clients maintain control over their data while contributing to model improvement.

Applications of Federated Learning

Federated Learning finds applications in various domains:

1. Healthcare

In healthcare, patient data privacy is crucial. Federated Learning allows medical institutions to collaborate on improving diagnostic models without sharing sensitive patient records.

2. Smart Devices

Smartphones and IoT devices can use Federated Learning to enhance predictive text, speech recognition, and personalized recommendations without transmitting user data to a central server.

3. Financial Services

Banks and financial institutions can use Federated Learning to develop fraud detection models while maintaining the privacy of transaction data.

Challenges and Considerations

Despite its advantages, Federated Learning faces challenges:

1. Communication Overhead

The process of transmitting model updates between clients and the central server can introduce communication overhead, especially in scenarios with many clients.

2. Heterogeneous Data

Clients may have heterogeneous data distributions, which can complicate model aggregation. Addressing this requires advanced techniques.

3. Security Risks

While Federated Learning mitigates some security risks, it introduces new ones, such as model inversion attacks or privacy leakage through model updates. Robust security measures are essential.

Future Directions

The future of Federated Learning hinges on overcoming its challenges and expanding its applicability. Researchers are actively working on improving model aggregation methods, addressing communication overhead, and enhancing security. As data privacy regulations become more stringent, Federated Learning is likely to gain further prominence as a privacy-preserving machine learning approach.

In conclusion, Federated Learning represents a significant advancement in machine learning, offering a way to harness the collective intelligence of decentralized data sources while preserving privacy and security. As this technology matures and overcomes its challenges, it has the potential to revolutionize various industries by enabling collaborative model training without compromising sensitive data.

Section 18.5: Ethical AI and Regulation

As artificial intelligence (AI) and machine learning (ML) technologies continue to advance and permeate various aspects of society, concerns about ethical AI and the need for regulation have become increasingly prominent. In this section, we'll explore the ethical considerations surrounding AI, the importance of responsible AI development, and the role of regulation in shaping the future of AI.

Ethical Considerations in AI

AI systems can have profound societal impacts, both positive and negative. It's essential to consider the ethical implications of AI technologies:

1. Bias and Fairness

AI systems can inherit biases from the data they are trained on, leading to unfair or discriminatory outcomes. Addressing bias in AI is a critical ethical concern, especially in areas like hiring, lending, and criminal justice.

2. Privacy

AI often involves processing vast amounts of personal data. Ensuring the privacy of individuals and safeguarding against data breaches is crucial.

3. Accountability

Determining responsibility when AI systems make mistakes or cause harm is challenging. Ethical AI requires clear lines of accountability.

4. Transparency and Explainability

AI models can be highly complex and challenging to interpret. Ensuring that AI decisions are transparent and explainable is essential for trust and accountability.

5. Job Displacement

AI has the potential to automate many tasks, which can lead to job displacement. Ethical considerations include retraining and upskilling the workforce.

Responsible AI Development

Developers and organizations must adopt principles of responsible AI development:

1. Ethical Guidelines

Organizations should establish ethical guidelines for AI development, addressing issues like bias, privacy, and transparency.

2. Bias Mitigation

Efforts should be made to identify and mitigate bias in AI systems, both in the data used for training and in the algorithms themselves.

3. Data Privacy

Strict data privacy measures, including data anonymization and encryption, should be implemented to protect user data.

4. User Consent

Users should have clear information about how AI systems use their data and the ability to provide informed consent.

5. Continuous Monitoring

AI systems should be continually monitored for biases, errors, and unintended consequences.

Role of Regulation

Given the global reach and potential risks of AI, governments and regulatory bodies are taking steps to develop AI-specific regulations:

1. Data Protection Regulations

Existing data protection regulations, like the European Union's General Data Protection Regulation (GDPR), play a role in governing AI applications by safeguarding user data.

2. Algorithmic Accountability

Proposed regulations may require organizations to explain and justify their AI algorithms' decisions, ensuring transparency and fairness.

3. Ethical AI Frameworks

Governments and industry organizations are developing frameworks for ethical AI development and usage.

4. Sector-Specific Regulations

Certain industries, such as healthcare and finance, may see sector-specific AI regulations to address unique challenges.

Challenges and Future Directions

The regulation of AI presents various challenges:

1. Rapid Technological Advancements

AI technologies evolve quickly, making it challenging for regulations to keep pace.

2. Global Consensus

AI operates across borders, making it challenging to establish uniform regulations globally.

3. Balancing Innovation and Safety

Regulations must strike a balance between fostering innovation and ensuring the safety and ethical use of AI.

4. Enforcement

Enforcing AI regulations, especially in a global context, can be complex and may require international cooperation.

In conclusion, ethical AI and regulation are intrinsically linked to ensuring that AI technologies benefit society while minimizing harm. Responsible AI development, guided by ethical principles, is essential for building trust and accountability. As AI continues to advance, governments, organizations, and the AI community must work together to create a regulatory framework that promotes innovation while safeguarding individuals and society from potential risks and harms. Ethical considerations and regulatory efforts will play a significant role in shaping the future of AI and its impact on the world.

Section 19.1: Books, Courses, and Online Resources

In the ever-evolving field of machine learning and artificial intelligence, staying up-to-date with the latest developments and expanding your knowledge is crucial. This section will explore various resources, including books, online courses, and other materials, that can help you deepen your understanding and excel in the field of machine learning.

Books

Books remain an invaluable resource for learning and mastering machine learning concepts. Here are some highly recommended books:

1. *"Introduction to Machine Learning with Python" by Andreas C. Müller & Sarah Guido*
   - This book provides a practical introduction to machine learning with Python, covering essential topics and libraries.

2. *"Pattern Recognition and Machine Learning" by Christopher M. Bishop*
   - Bishop's book is a comprehensive resource on pattern recognition and machine learning, suitable for both beginners and experts.

3. *"Deep Learning" by Ian Goodfellow, Yoshua Bengio, and Aaron Courville*
   - Dive deep into the world of deep learning with this authoritative book, often referred to as the "Deep Learning Bible."

4. *"Python Machine Learning" by Sebastian Raschka and Vahid Mirjalili*
   - This book offers practical insights into machine learning with Python, including hands-on examples and real-world applications.

5. *"Hands-On Machine Learning with Scikit-Learn, Keras, and TensorFlow" by Aurélien Géron*
   - Géron's book is a practical guide to machine learning, covering popular libraries like Scikit-Learn, Keras, and TensorFlow.

Online Courses

Online courses provide flexibility and access to expert-led instruction. Here are some renowned online courses for machine learning:

1. *Coursera Machine Learning (Stanford University)*
   - Taught by Andrew Ng, this course is a popular choice for beginners and covers fundamental machine learning concepts.

2. *Deep Learning Specialization (Coursera)*
   - Also by Andrew Ng, this specialization delves into deep learning, covering neural networks, CNNs, RNNs, and more.

7. AI and ML Conferences

Attending conferences and workshops dedicated to artificial intelligence and machine learning is an excellent way to engage with the community. While major conferences like NeurIPS and ICML draw thousands of participants, there are also regional and specialized conferences that cater to specific interests within the field.

8. Online Learning Platforms

Online learning platforms such as Coursera, edX, and Udacity often include discussion forums where learners can interact with peers, ask questions, and share insights related to machine learning courses. Engaging in these forums can enhance your learning experience and help you connect with fellow learners.

9. Social Media

Social media platforms like Twitter and LinkedIn offer opportunities to follow prominent figures in the machine learning community, including researchers, practitioners, and organizations. By following and engaging with these individuals, you can stay updated on the latest research, trends, and discussions in the field.

Joining machine learning communities not only fosters collaboration and knowledge sharing but also provides a sense of belonging in a rapidly growing and evolving field. Whether you're a beginner looking to learn or an experienced practitioner seeking to stay current, participating in these communities can be instrumental in your machine learning journey. Remember to be respectful, contribute positively, and take advantage of the wealth of knowledge available within these communities.

Section 19.3: Keeping Up with the Latest Research

Machine learning is a rapidly evolving field with new research papers, techniques, and advancements emerging regularly. Staying updated with the latest research is crucial for both newcomers and experienced practitioners. In this section, we will explore strategies and resources to help you keep up with the ever-changing landscape of machine learning research.

1. ArXiv and Preprint Servers

ArXiv.org is a popular platform for researchers to share preprints of their papers, including those in the field of machine learning. Subscribing to relevant categories or keywords on ArXiv allows you to receive notifications when new papers are uploaded. Additionally, other preprint servers like bioRxiv and ChemRxiv may contain interdisciplinary research relevant to machine learning applications in various domains.

2. Academic Journals

Machine learning-related journals publish research articles, reviews, and surveys on a regular basis. Journals like the Journal of Machine Learning Research (JMLR), Machine Learning, and the International Journal of Machine Learning and Cybernetics provide valuable insights. Consider subscribing to these journals or checking their websites for the latest publications.

3. Conferences and Workshops

Machine learning conferences, such as NeurIPS, ICML, CVPR, and ACL, are premier venues for presenting and discussing cutting-edge research. Following conference proceedings and attending workshops can provide access to the latest breakthroughs and ideas. Many conferences also make their proceedings freely available online.

4. ResearchGate and Google Scholar

ResearchGate and Google Scholar are platforms that allow researchers to share their work and profiles. You can follow researchers, institutions, or specific topics on these platforms to receive updates on new publications and citations related to machine learning.

5. Blogs and Newsletters

Several blogs and newsletters focus on summarizing and explaining recent machine learning research. Subscribing to these sources, such as "Distill" and "The Morning Paper," can help you digest complex research papers and understand their implications.

6. Podcasts and YouTube Channels

Podcasts like "Machine Learning Street Talk" and YouTube channels like "Two Minute Papers" offer audio and video content that discusses recent research in an accessible format. These platforms are ideal for learning about the latest trends and innovations on the go.

7. Social Media and Online Communities

Platforms like Twitter and Reddit have active machine learning communities that share and discuss research papers. By following relevant hashtags, researchers, and discussion threads, you can stay informed about trending topics and papers in the field.

8. Research Labs and Organizations

Many machine learning research labs and organizations, such as OpenAI, DeepMind, and Google AI, regularly release papers and blog posts about their work. Subscribing to their blogs or newsletters can provide insights into the latest research and developments.

9. Online Courses and Specializations

Online learning platforms like Coursera, edX, and Udacity offer courses and specializations in machine learning. These often include content on the latest research trends and techniques. Enrolling in such courses can help you learn and apply the most recent advancements.

10. Peer Discussion Groups

Forming or joining peer discussion groups or journal clubs with colleagues or fellow learners can be an effective way to collectively review and discuss recent research papers. These groups can help you understand complex concepts and identify practical applications.

Remember that keeping up with the latest research in machine learning is an ongoing process. It's essential to develop a personalized strategy that aligns with your specific interests and goals. Whether you prefer reading academic papers, watching video summaries, or engaging in discussions, staying updated will enhance your knowledge and skills in this dynamic field.

Section 19.4: Building Your Machine Learning Portfolio

Building a strong machine learning portfolio is a crucial step if you want to establish yourself as a competent machine learning practitioner or data scientist. A well-structured portfolio not only showcases your skills but also helps you stand out to potential employers or collaborators. In this section, we'll explore the key elements of creating an effective machine learning portfolio.

1. Select Diverse Projects

When building your portfolio, aim to include a variety of machine learning projects that demonstrate your expertise in different areas. This could include projects related to natural language processing, computer vision, time series analysis, and more. Diversity in your portfolio shows that you have a broad skill set and can tackle various types of problems.

2. Highlight Real-World Applications

Choose projects with real-world applications or practical relevance. Employers and collaborators are often interested in how your skills can be applied to solve actual problems. Explain the context of each project and how it addresses a specific issue or provides value.

3. Provide Clear Documentation

Clear and concise documentation is essential for your portfolio projects. Include detailed explanations of the problem, your approach, the dataset used, and the results achieved. Use markdown or dedicated portfolio platforms to format your documentation neatly.

4. Share Code Repositories

Upload your project code to platforms like GitHub or GitLab. These platforms allow you to showcase your coding skills, version control practices, and collaboration abilities. Ensure that your code is well-organized, commented, and includes README files for easy understanding.

5. Display Visualizations and Results

Incorporate visualizations and results to make your portfolio visually appealing. Use tools like Matplotlib, Seaborn, or Plotly to create informative graphs and charts that help explain your work. Visuals can quickly convey the impact of your projects.

6. Explain Your Process

Detail your workflow and the steps you followed in each project. This should include data preprocessing, feature engineering, model selection, training, evaluation, and any iterations. Explain how you made decisions and improved your models.

7. Showcase Model Performance

Highlight the performance metrics and evaluation results for your machine learning models. Include metrics like accuracy, precision, recall, F1-score, or relevant domain-specific metrics. Comparing your models to baseline models or other benchmarks can add context.

8. Include Personal Projects

In addition to showcasing academic or work-related projects, consider including personal projects that reflect your passion for machine learning. These could be projects related to your hobbies or interests, demonstrating your commitment to continuous learning.

9. Share Challenges and Learning

Don't shy away from discussing challenges, failures, or limitations you encountered during your projects. Demonstrating how you learned from setbacks and adapted your approach can show resilience and problem-solving skills.

10. Keep It Updated

Regularly update your portfolio with new projects and accomplishments. The machine learning field evolves rapidly, so staying current is essential. As you complete new projects or acquire new skills, add them to your portfolio to reflect your progress.

11. Seek Feedback

Before finalizing your portfolio, consider seeking feedback from peers, mentors, or online communities. Constructive criticism can help you improve the presentation and content of your projects.

12. Make It Accessible

Ensure that your portfolio is easily accessible online. You can host it on platforms like GitHub Pages, Netlify, or create a personal website. Make sure it's well-optimized for mobile devices and loads quickly.

13. Personalize Your Story

Lastly, add a personal touch to your portfolio. Share your motivation for pursuing machine learning, your background, and what excites you about this field. A brief bio can help humanize your portfolio and connect with viewers.

Remember that your machine learning portfolio is a dynamic representation of your skills and growth. As you gain more experience and tackle new challenges, your portfolio will evolve to reflect your expertise and interests. It's an ongoing tool for showcasing your journey in the world of machine learning.

Section 19.5: Career Opportunities in Machine Learning

Machine learning is a dynamic and rapidly growing field with a wide range of career opportunities. Whether you're just starting your journey in machine learning or looking to advance your career, understanding the various roles and industries where machine learning is applied can help you make informed decisions. In this section, we'll explore the diverse career opportunities available in machine learning.

1. Machine Learning Engineer

Machine Learning Engineers are responsible for designing, developing, and implementing machine learning solutions. They work on building and deploying machine learning models, optimizing algorithms, and integrating them into production systems. A strong background in programming, data engineering, and model deployment is crucial for this role.

2. Data Scientist

Data Scientists leverage data to gain insights and make data-driven decisions. They use statistical analysis, machine learning, and data visualization techniques to extract valuable information from large datasets. Data Scientists work in various domains, including healthcare, finance, marketing, and more.

3. AI Researcher

AI Researchers focus on advancing the field of artificial intelligence through cutting-edge research. They explore new algorithms, develop innovative models, and contribute to academic and industry publications. This role often requires a deep understanding of machine learning theory and mathematics.

4. Natural Language Processing (NLP) Engineer

NLP Engineers specialize in the development of natural language processing models and applications. They work on tasks such as sentiment analysis, chatbots, language translation, and speech recognition. Proficiency in NLP libraries like NLTK, spaCy, or Hugging Face Transformers is essential.

5. Computer Vision Engineer

Computer Vision Engineers focus on developing computer vision applications. They work on tasks like image classification, object detection, facial recognition, and autonomous vehicle perception. Knowledge of computer vision libraries such as OpenCV and deep learning frameworks like TensorFlow or PyTorch is vital.

6. Data Engineer

Data Engineers build and maintain the infrastructure for collecting, storing, and processing data. They work closely with Data Scientists and Machine Learning Engineers to ensure that data is accessible and ready for analysis. Skills in databases, data pipelines, and cloud computing are valuable in this role.

7. AI Product Manager

AI Product Managers bridge the gap between technical teams and business goals. They define the strategy for AI and machine learning products, prioritize features, and collaborate with development teams to ensure successful product launches. Strong project management and communication skills are essential.

8. Machine Learning Operations (MLOps) Engineer

MLOps Engineers focus on the deployment and management of machine learning models in production. They build automation pipelines, monitor model performance, and ensure scalability and reliability. Proficiency in DevOps practices and containerization technologies like Docker and Kubernetes is crucial.

9. AI Ethics and Fairness Researcher

As AI and machine learning become more pervasive, the need for ethical AI practices grows. AI Ethics Researchers work on ensuring fairness, transparency, and accountability in AI systems. They develop guidelines, conduct audits, and promote responsible AI development.

10. Industry-Specific Roles

Machine learning is applied in various industries, including healthcare, finance, e-commerce, autonomous vehicles, and more. Each industry offers unique career opportunities. For example, you can become a Healthcare Data Analyst, Quantitative Analyst in Finance, or Computer Vision Engineer in Robotics.

11. Start Your Own Venture

If you have a groundbreaking machine learning idea or application, you might consider starting your own company or joining a startup. Entrepreneurship in AI can lead to innovative solutions and significant impact.

12. Academia and Research Institutions

If you're passionate about research and education, you can pursue a career in academia or research institutions. This path involves conducting research, publishing papers, and educating the next generation of machine learning professionals.

13. Freelancing and Consulting

Freelancing or consulting as a machine learning expert can provide flexibility and the opportunity to work on diverse projects. Many organizations seek external experts to help solve specific machine learning challenges.

14. Government and Nonprofits

Government agencies and nonprofit organizations often employ machine learning professionals to address societal issues, such as healthcare access, environmental conservation, and social justice.

15. Continuous Learning and Networking

Regardless of your career path, continuous learning is essential in the ever-evolving field of machine learning. Attend conferences, workshops, and online courses to stay updated. Networking with professionals in the field can open doors to new opportunities.

Machine learning offers a wide array of career paths, and the demand for skilled professionals continues to grow. Whether you're interested in research, development, or applying machine learning to specific industries, there are numerous opportunities to make a meaningful impact in this exciting field. Your career in machine learning can be as diverse as the applications of AI itself.

Chapter 20: Conclusion and Beyond

Section 20.1: Recap of the Journey

As we reach the final chapter of this book, it's a good time to reflect on the journey you've taken through the vast landscape of machine learning. You've delved into fundamental concepts, explored practical techniques, and gained insights into various applications of this exciting field. Let's recap the key highlights and takeaways from your journey.

1. **Understanding Machine Learning**: You started with the basics, grasping the core concepts of machine learning and its significance in today's world. You learned how

it differs from traditional programming and the various types of machine learning tasks.

2. **Python for Machine Learning**: Python emerged as your primary programming language for machine learning. You set up your Python environment and acquired essential Python skills necessary for working with data and building models.

3. **Data Preprocessing and Exploration**: Data is the foundation of machine learning. You explored techniques for cleaning, transforming, and exploring datasets. You also learned how to handle categorical data and perform exploratory data analysis (EDA).

4. **Supervised Learning**: You delved into supervised learning, understanding both regression and classification tasks. Linear regression, decision trees, logistic regression, and support vector machines became part of your toolkit.

5. **Unsupervised Learning and Dimensionality Reduction**: Clustering techniques like K-Means and hierarchical clustering helped you uncover patterns in unlabeled data. You also learned about dimensionality reduction methods like PCA and t-SNE.

6. **Model Selection and Hyperparameter Tuning**: To build effective models, you explored techniques for model selection and hyperparameter tuning. Cross-validation, grid search, and best practices for tuning were covered.

7. **Ensemble Learning**: You discovered the power of ensemble methods, including bagging and boosting. Techniques like AdaBoost and Gradient Boosting became essential tools for improving model performance.

8. **Neural Networks and Deep Learning**: The world of deep learning opened up as you explored neural networks, CNNs, and RNNs. You built and trained deep learning models and explored their applications.

9. **Natural Language Processing (NLP)**: NLP introduced you to the world of text data. You learned about text preprocessing, building text classification models, and even delved into word embeddings and sentiment analysis.

10. **Computer Vision**: The field of computer vision allowed you to work with image data. You built image classification models, explored object detection, and harnessed the power of transfer learning.

11. **Time Series Analysis**: Time series data presented its unique challenges. You learned how to handle time series data, decompose it, and build forecasting models using techniques like ARIMA and Prophet.

12. **Reinforcement Learning**: The exciting world of reinforcement learning was introduced, where you explored Q-learning, deep Q-networks, and policy gradients for solving complex decision-making problems.

13. **Model Deployment**: You gained insights into deploying machine learning models into production, including building RESTful APIs, containerization, and cloud deployment. You also learned about monitoring and scaling models.

14. **Ethics and Bias**: Ethical considerations in machine learning became a critical topic. You explored bias mitigation techniques and responsible AI development.

15. **Real-World Projects**: You understood the development lifecycle of real-world machine learning projects, from choosing the right project to data collection, model building, and deployment.

16. **Case Studies**: Industry case studies highlighted the practical applications of machine learning in healthcare, finance, e-commerce, autonomous vehicles, and more.

17. **Future Trends**: You glimpsed into the future of machine learning, exploring trends such as Explainable AI (XAI), Quantum Machine Learning, Federated Learning, and the role of ethical AI regulation.

18. **Resources and Further Learning**: You were provided with guidance on resources, communities, research, building a portfolio, and exploring career opportunities in machine learning.

Key Takeaways

Throughout your journey, you've acquired a rich set of skills and knowledge in machine learning, making you well-prepared to tackle real-world challenges and contribute to the field. Here are some key takeaways:

- Machine learning is a vast field with diverse applications, and continuous learning is essential to stay updated.
- Python is a versatile language for machine learning, and libraries like NumPy, pandas, scikit-learn, and TensorFlow are valuable tools.
- Data is at the heart of machine learning, and data preprocessing is a crucial step in any project.
- Model selection, hyperparameter tuning, and ensembling techniques can significantly improve model performance.
- Deep learning has revolutionized many domains, including NLP, computer vision, and reinforcement learning.
- Ethical considerations, fairness, and transparency are critical aspects of AI development.
- Real-world projects and case studies provide practical experience and insights into industry applications.
- The machine learning community and resources for further learning are vast and accessible.

As you conclude this book, remember that machine learning is a field that continually evolves. New algorithms, techniques, and applications emerge regularly. Embrace a lifelong learning mindset, stay curious, and continue to explore and contribute to the world of machine learning.

**Your Role

Section 20.2: Key Takeaways

As we conclude this book, it's essential to summarize the key takeaways from your journey in the world of machine learning. These insights will serve as a guide for your future endeavors in this exciting field:

1. **Diverse Applications**: Machine learning finds applications in various domains, including healthcare, finance, e-commerce, autonomous vehicles, and more. Recognize the potential for ML to solve real-world problems in diverse industries.

2. **Python Proficiency**: Python is the preferred language for machine learning due to its versatility and rich ecosystem of libraries. Continue honing your Python skills, especially in libraries like NumPy, pandas, scikit-learn, and TensorFlow.

3. **Data Preprocessing**: Data is the foundation of ML. Data preprocessing, including cleaning, transformation, and exploration, is critical for building accurate models. Pay meticulous attention to data quality and understand your data thoroughly.

4. **Model Building and Evaluation**: Model selection, hyperparameter tuning, and ensembling techniques can significantly impact model performance. Experiment with different algorithms and hyperparameters, and use cross-validation for robust evaluation.

5. **Deep Learning**: Deep learning, powered by neural networks, has transformed many ML domains. Explore deep learning further, especially in areas like computer vision, natural language processing, and reinforcement learning.

6. **Ethical AI**: Consider the ethical implications of your ML projects. Be aware of bias and fairness issues, and use mitigation techniques to ensure responsible AI development.

7. **Real-World Projects**: Building and deploying real-world ML projects is invaluable. Choose projects that align with your interests and learn by doing. Projects provide practical experience and demonstrate your skills to potential employers or collaborators.

8. **Community and Resources**: Join machine learning communities, attend conferences, and engage with researchers and practitioners. Stay updated with the

latest research and industry trends. Utilize online courses, books, and tutorials to continue learning.

9. **Lifelong Learning**: Machine learning is a dynamic field that evolves rapidly. Embrace a lifelong learning mindset. Keep exploring new concepts, techniques, and emerging trends to stay at the forefront of ML advancements.

10. **Your Impact**: Recognize the potential impact of your work. Machine learning has the power to drive innovation and solve complex problems, making a positive difference in society. Consider your role in advancing AI and ML responsibly.

In conclusion, your journey in machine learning is just beginning. The knowledge and skills you've acquired in this book are the foundation upon which you can build a fulfilling and impactful career in machine learning. Stay curious, keep learning, and continue pushing the boundaries of what's possible in this exciting field. Your contributions to the world of AI and ML have the potential to shape the future.

Section 20.3: Embracing a Lifelong Learning Mindset

The field of machine learning and artificial intelligence is marked by rapid advancements and constant innovation. As we wrap up this book, it's crucial to emphasize the importance of embracing a lifelong learning mindset. The journey you've embarked upon is not a one-time endeavor but an ongoing exploration of a dynamic and evolving field. Here are some key points to consider:

1. Continuous Learning Is Essential

Machine learning is constantly evolving. New algorithms, techniques, and libraries emerge regularly. To stay relevant, you must commit to continuous learning. This might involve taking online courses, attending workshops, reading research papers, or simply experimenting with new tools and technologies.

2. Stay Informed About Industry Trends

The machine learning landscape is heavily influenced by industry trends. Keeping up with these trends is crucial for career growth. Follow AI and ML news, blogs, and forums to understand how the field is evolving and what skills are in demand.

3. Contribute to Open Source Projects

Contributing to open source projects is an excellent way to learn and collaborate with the broader ML community. It allows you to work on real-world projects, gain experience, and make valuable connections.

4. Collaborate and Network

Machine learning is a collaborative field. Engage with others in the community, attend conferences, join meetups, and participate in online forums. Collaborative projects and networking can lead to new opportunities and insights.

5. Mentorship and Teaching

Consider mentoring others who are starting their journey in machine learning. Teaching and explaining concepts to others can deepen your understanding and help solidify your knowledge.

6. Experiment and Innovate

Don't be afraid to experiment and innovate. Create your projects, explore new ideas, and push the boundaries of what's possible. Innovation often arises from thinking outside the box and taking risks.

7. Ethical Considerations

As machine learning becomes more integrated into society, ethical considerations become paramount. Stay informed about ethical AI practices and contribute to the responsible development of AI systems.

8. Portfolio Development

Building a portfolio of projects is an excellent way to showcase your skills to potential employers or collaborators. Keep adding new projects that demonstrate your capabilities and interests.

9. Career Advancement

If you're pursuing a career in machine learning, set clear goals for advancement. Whether it's becoming a machine learning engineer, researcher, or data scientist, define your path and work toward it.

10. Impact on Society

Remember the impact your work can have on society. Aim to contribute positively to the world through your machine learning projects. Address real-world problems and consider the broader implications of your work.

In summary, the field of machine learning offers endless possibilities for growth and impact. Embracing a lifelong learning mindset is not just a choice but a necessity to thrive in this dynamic field. Stay curious, stay committed, and keep pushing the boundaries of what you can achieve with machine learning. Your journey has the potential to lead to groundbreaking discoveries and innovations that shape the future of AI and ML.

Section 20.4: Your Role in Advancing AI and ML

As we conclude this book, it's essential to reflect on your role in advancing the fields of Artificial Intelligence (AI) and Machine Learning (ML). Whether you're a novice or an experienced practitioner, your contributions matter, and you can play a part in shaping the future of AI and ML. Here are some key considerations:

1. Problem Solving with AI/ML

One of the primary roles you can undertake is that of a problem solver. AI and ML are powerful tools for addressing complex challenges across various domains, from healthcare to finance to environmental science. Identify problems that matter to you and explore how AI and ML can be applied to find solutions.

2. Research and Innovation

If you have a passion for pushing the boundaries of knowledge, consider engaging in research and innovation. Researchers in AI and ML drive the field forward by developing new algorithms, models, and techniques. Whether in academia or industry, your research contributions can have a lasting impact.

3. Education and Mentorship

Share your knowledge and expertise with others. Becoming an educator or mentor allows you to empower the next generation of AI and ML practitioners. Teaching can help you deepen your understanding of the subject while helping others learn.

4. Ethical Leadership

Advocate for ethical AI and ML practices. Be aware of the ethical implications of your work and contribute to discussions about responsible AI development. By championing ethical principles, you can help ensure AI benefits society rather than harms it.

5. Interdisciplinary Collaboration

AI and ML are inherently interdisciplinary fields. Collaborate with experts from other domains, such as biology, psychology, or engineering, to tackle complex problems that require diverse perspectives. These collaborations often lead to innovative solutions.

6. Open Source Contributions

Contribute to open-source projects and communities. Open source plays a vital role in the democratization of AI and ML. By sharing code, tools, and knowledge, you can help accelerate progress and make AI more accessible to everyone.

7. Diverse and Inclusive AI

Promote diversity and inclusivity in AI and ML. Encourage underrepresented groups to enter the field and participate actively in initiatives that aim to address diversity issues. Diverse perspectives lead to more robust and fair AI systems.

8. Advocacy and Policy

Stay informed about AI-related policies and regulations. Advocate for responsible AI policies at the local, national, and international levels. Your involvement can help shape the legal and ethical frameworks that govern AI.

9. Real-World Applications

Focus on real-world applications. While theoretical research is essential, practical applications drive tangible impact. Work on projects that can be deployed to solve pressing issues and improve people's lives.

10. Lifelong Learning

Continuously upgrade your skills and knowledge. The AI and ML fields evolve rapidly, and staying up-to-date is crucial. Invest in lifelong learning to remain relevant and effective in your contributions.

Remember that your journey in AI and ML is part of a broader community effort to harness the potential of these technologies responsibly and ethically. Your contributions, no matter how big or small, contribute to the collective progress of AI and ML, making the world a better place through innovation and problem-solving. Keep exploring, keep learning, and keep advancing AI and ML for the benefit of all.

Section 20.5: Looking Ahead to the Future of ML

As we conclude this book, it's essential to look ahead to the future of Machine Learning (ML). ML is a dynamic field, constantly evolving and advancing. Here are some key trends and developments to watch for in the coming years:

1. Explainable AI (XAI)

Explainable AI is gaining traction as the demand for transparency and accountability in ML systems grows. Researchers are developing techniques to make ML models more interpretable and understandable, which is crucial for applications in healthcare, finance, and law.

2. Quantum Machine Learning

Quantum computing promises to revolutionize ML by solving complex problems exponentially faster than classical computers. ML algorithms designed for quantum computers are expected to lead to breakthroughs in optimization, cryptography, and drug discovery.

3. Federated Learning

Federated Learning allows model training across decentralized devices while keeping data localized. It's a privacy-preserving approach that's gaining importance in applications like healthcare, where data privacy is critical.

4. Ethical AI and Regulation

As AI systems become more integrated into society, governments and organizations are developing regulations and guidelines for ethical AI development and deployment. This includes addressing issues related to bias, fairness, and accountability.

5. AutoML and Democratization

AutoML tools are making it easier for non-experts to create ML models. This democratization of ML empowers individuals and organizations to leverage ML for a wide range of applications without deep technical expertise.

6. Natural Language Processing Advancements

NLP continues to advance, with more sophisticated language models like GPT-4 and beyond. These models have the potential to enable more natural and context-aware interactions between humans and machines.

7. AI in Healthcare

AI is poised to transform healthcare with applications in diagnosis, drug discovery, and personalized treatment plans. ML models can analyze medical images, predict disease outbreaks, and assist in drug development.

8. AI in Climate Science

ML is increasingly used to analyze climate data and develop models for climate prediction and mitigation. ML-driven climate models can help us better understand and address the challenges of climate change.

9. AI in Robotics and Autonomous Systems

Advancements in AI are driving the development of more capable and autonomous robots and drones. These technologies have applications in areas such as manufacturing, agriculture, and transportation.

10. AI for Social Good

The AI community is increasingly focused on using ML for social good, tackling issues like poverty, education, and public health. ML-driven initiatives are helping address some of the world's most pressing challenges.

11. Human-Machine Collaboration

The future of ML is likely to involve closer collaboration between humans and machines. ML systems that can complement human skills and decision-making are expected to become more common.

12. Edge AI

Edge computing, where AI processing happens on local devices rather than in the cloud, is gaining prominence. This is particularly important for applications like autonomous vehicles and IoT devices.

13. Continuous Learning

ML models that can adapt and learn continuously from new data are becoming more important. This allows models to stay relevant and accurate in a changing world.

14. AI in Creativity

AI is increasingly being used in creative fields like art, music, and literature. Generative models can assist artists and creators in generating new content.

15. Global Collaboration

The global nature of AI research and development means that collaboration among researchers, organizations, and governments is essential. International cooperation can help address ethical, security, and regulatory challenges.

The future of ML is bright and filled with opportunities for innovation and positive impact. As you continue your journey in this field, stay curious, keep learning, and be open to exploring new ideas and technologies. Your contributions can help shape the future of ML and make the world a better place through the power of intelligent machines.

www.ingramcontent.com/pod-product-compliance
Lightning Source LLC
LaVergne TN
LVHW051324050326
832903LV00031B/3353